Claudia Fraimeau

Field Notes from Grief:
The First Year

Printed in the United States of America.
ISBN: 9781595717535
Library of Congress Control Number: 2011942776

Designed by
War Admiral Press

Published by
Word Association Publishers
205 Fifth Avenue
Tarentum, Pennsylvania 15084

www.wordassociation.com
1.800.827.7903

Cover Art by Claudia Giannini

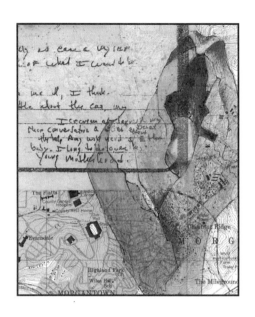

Field Notes from Grief:

The First Year

Judith Gold Stitzel

with artwork by
Claudia Giannini

With gratitude to my husband Bob, to all who loved him,
and to everything he loved.

With love for David, Laurel and Kaya,
who carry him in their hearts.

left its perch where I overlooked & looked another
floats shadow where its legs might be
creature entirely as it swims no legs visible at
all. Gulls call across the sky.

A blue promise beyond despite grey puffs the sun
an equinimeow ball

"Equinimeow, is that a word?"
"I never heard it before."
"Doesn't mean it's not a word."
"I think it from equanimity."
"Maybe. But that's a noun."
"I know it's a noun."
"Let's check the dictionary."
"We don't have a dictionary. We're in the country."
"Why should that matter what the dictionary says."
"I like it."
"what do you like..."
"The sound of it. Equinimeow ball."
though she said Equinimeow thous
"But what if it's not a word?"
I invented one / "Oh."
"See—"
"that's not kosher."
"what do you really have to do it."
"Look up."
"where"
"In the vertiginous sky."
"Mmm, that doesn't make any sense at all."

Preface

I have kept journals since the mid-1960s and continued to do so, both during and after the fifteen months my husband lived with stomach cancer. Bob died in September 2007. *Field Notes from Grief: The First Year* was shaped from the journals I kept the year after his death (introduced by the two weeks that preceded it). But without my collaborator, Claudia Giannini, whose thirteen color images accompany the text, there would have been no book.

Claudia and I had talked tentatively years earlier about another project which would have brought her images and my words together—a journal about my garden—but that never came to fruition. And then, mid-way during the year following Bob's death, as I was absorbing my new reality and finding a new place in the world, Claudia suggested we try again to work together.

Early on in the process, we photocopied journal pages from each of the months following Bob's death and chose one from each month to form the center of each image. We chose them not for readability, but for "shape," some having only writing, some having scribbled notes such as phone numbers and to-do lists. Using these, Claudia created visual responses to my words. Sometimes we would discuss her work as she was in the middle of it, with me asking questions and making suggestions. Other times, she would show me finished compositions.

We knew from the beginning that we wanted to make something beautiful. But it took a while before I fully accepted that my pages were valuable not only as a stimulus for her haunting images, but for what they had to say to others. When I moved from the private to the public realm, editing became a necessity, a challenge, and a release. Editing the journals to share them, I strove to maintain the spontaneity, contradictions and, even confusion, of the original; through reading and re-reading them I found the threads that hold them and me together.

August

8/24/07   Bob has lost 25 pounds. Loss of fluid? Loss of flesh? Is he
eating himself?

I imagine myself no longer eating anything that can't be eaten
easily in bed, lying next to him. Bananas, for instance. Or a bowl
of cottage cheese. Sliced tomatoes in mayonnaise. A bagel is tricky
because of the crumbs.

In the course of a marriage, when a husband asks, "Do we have any
cheerios?" the wife may hear, "Why haven't you put the cheerios on
the table?" When Bob asked, I heard, "I'm feeling well enough to
eat," and the *we* was a precious affirmation.

What else should I be doing? Getting Bob to the hospital for
hydration? Intravenous feeding? Which statement is true: *Nothing
I do matters anymore,* or *I'm the only one who can keep him alive?*

I'm trying to make sense of the Advantra insurance benefits, only
to realize that we may have major medical bills before long.

To relax, I read a story in *The New Yorker*. I admire the
narrative control.

8/25/07   On our deck, with Bob asleep beside me, I imagine I could be
content living with my dead mate, his presence giving shape and
rhythm to my life. This could be enough, sitting near, writing, our
garden below; occasionally I could go inside—perhaps to get a
blanket—even do short errands, and return to find him, waiting.
I'm thinking wildly, I know. The only sleep short of death would be
a coma, implying care and confusion, fear and frustration, nurses,
doctors, tubes—my being utterly alone, while surrounded.

4

8/26/07   In the middle of the night, Bob tripped over a rug on the way to the bathroom. No bones broken. No blood. It could have been worse. Words traipse through my mind as I try to sleep again:

Because I am too weak for irony
and too stubborn for hope
I try to be content with gratitude.
But to tell the truth,
I am sick and tired of gratitude
for the little things
I need so desperately
because I am sick and tired.

What's different now, after fifteen months, is that we are not working as a team anymore. He doesn't always know what he wants. He doesn't know what's good for him.

Contradictions tumble everywhere. One moment I'm dedicating myself to Bob forever, whatever state he's in—just let him live— then I see myself alone in South Australia, where Bob and I lived years ago. Ah . . . . the white sand, the ocean foam, the scent of almond blossoms.

As I write in my journal, old voices intrude: "What makes you think you're experiencing something no one else has? That no one else has written about?"

8/27/07   He's been admitted to the hospital to have fluid drained. It seems the drugs he was taking may have stopped working. On the way to his room, I push him in a wheelchair, the first time it's been necessary. When we pass someone we know, he points his thumb downward.

What's going on? I refuse to take him home until I understand what's happening, what we might expect, and what will be my role. As caretaker. As advocate. As wife. But I'm not in a hurry. As long as I don't know the worst, if and how far the cancer has spread, I can sit here with Bob asleep, knowing I am not fully responsible. We are both relatively safe and relatively alive.

8/28/07   There are cancer cells in the abdominal fluid, but the doctors convince me Bob would do better at home while we wait for new drugs to kick in. New drugs! I shoot into the air from almost drowning, exploding into life again. But, very soon, fear slimes my body like seaweed.

There will be so much to do when Bob dies. Things he took care of. Insurance. Taxes. Plumbing. The car. Won't everything I've been putting on hold come tumbling down once the bulwark of hope has crumbled?

8/30/07   Being home is hard for both of us.

"This is the worst day of my life."

That's what Bob said and I fear his words will echo through the rest of mine.

He is hiccupping and throwing up. I think it's bile and I tell that to the nurse when I call to get advice. She recommends I watch him closely and keep her informed. But what's the point when there is no more life in the man? At what point should we say, "Okay, we're on the last road, no more switchbacks?" When he was first diagnosed, Bob told me he wanted everything done to keep him alive, including any emergency surgery, however unlikely its success. I was grateful for his clarity. But what did he want *now*? Did he anticipate being this miserable?

He's not himself or—even worse—enough himself to know that any illusion that we could beat this thing is finally—finally—gone.

Judith, can we go to bed now?
Can I do anything for you?

Talk.
What should I say?

No, no. Me. I don't want to go to the hospital. I feel safe here.
Even when I'm not sure what I'm doing?

Yes.

September

9/2/07   I told Bob we would not go to the hospital unless I couldn't handle things. In the end, I couldn't handle things. While sitting on the back deck, he became so weak and heavy in my arms, I barely got him inside and onto our bed. Dr. A had given me his cell phone number, but I couldn't get through. After several desperate tries, I called 911. Three hours in the emergency room until a bed on the cancer floor became free; two hours more before he died.

Could we have done more? Something different? Before the ambulance carried him from our home, Bob asked that I bring a change of clothes for him to come home in. I took his favorite Lands' End shirt. Maybe he didn't think he was dying. But wasn't that a tear I saw in the emergency room? Rolling down his cheek behind the breathing apparatus?

The next morning you wake up.
You didn't die.
In the long in-betweens
you woke again
and again
ashamed
astonished
alive.
You didn't die
of grief.

Throughout the night, the death scene replays. In a continuous loop, the unbelievable and the unbearable mix. "Code blue, code blue." The crash cart enters, as if from a TV show. Dr. A's voice: "I don't think you want that code. Nothing can stop the bleeding. We can make him comfortable." He ushers me out of the room, finds a chair for me, kneels next to me. A nurse puts a warm blanket around my shoulders. Young Dr. C, on call that evening, sits on the floor beside me.

"I tried so hard," I say, sobbing.

"You both did everything you could," Dr. A says. "Cancer is a cruel disease."

"How long will he live?" I ask. I will stay by his side as long as necessary.

"We never know—minutes, hours."

A nurse comes out and doesn't need to say a word.

When I return to the room, what I notice first is a blanket rolled beneath Bob's chin to keep his mouth from falling open. Who should I thank for that courtesy? I sit on the bed and take his hand in mine. I lean over to kiss his forehead. I say thank-you. I say I love you. I say good night.

Our dear friends Sharon and Irv arrive, though I don't remember calling them. They follow me back into the room, and with them near, I can say the word—*good-bye*. They will take me to their home for this first night alone. But what will I do with the rest of my life?

9/3/07   Friends come to our house to prepare it for a modified shiva observance. Anna removes what I could no longer see: grocery bags full of tissues, half-empty glasses of water and Ensure littering the rooms, a dirty kitchen floor. Maggie barely stifles a laugh when I say, "I'm not at the top of my game." She releases a memory of Bob and me laughing when, alluding to a half-hearted attempt to take the vegetable route to recovery, he had asked, "What if I'd drunk more cabbage juice?"

Different friends take care of me in different ways. Some feel I should respect the wisdom of the shiva rituals and allow myself to be cared for. When I get up from my chair to greet someone, they are firm. "Sit down." "You're not the host." Another protects me differently. "Let her get up and be with her guests. That's what she likes to do."

9/4/07   Give or take some miscounting, some 200 people came to the house to pay their respects.

9/5/07   Bob and I had arranged to give our bodies for medical research to the university for which we worked. Coming out of the anatomical gift office, I run into Dr. C dressed in "civies," a long skirt, thick belt, crisp white and blue shirt. We embrace. She tells me that when she arrived home the night Bob died, she was stunned by how quickly everything happened. "With this kind of cancer," she says, "it could have been longer and harder." She tells me that she looked into a clear night of stars and felt blessed. "We were lucky," she says. "I don't feel lucky—or blessed," I say, immediately embarrassed by my linguistic purity in the face of her kindness.

Later, I visit the nurses at the cancer center where Bob was lovingly cared for. Serious Beth hugs me the hardest, followed by Tammy, who tells me he was her favorite, then Abby who often joked with him about the diuretic and the "good chair" near the bathroom.

Dr. A comforts me. There had been a massive, unstoppable bleed. Confirmed by the final pathology report. "He's in heaven now," he says. I didn't tell him I don't believe in heaven. Earlier, one of the nurses said, "At least he's in a better place." "I don't know about that," I said, "but he was in a hell of a good one here."

After my visit, I allow myself a break at Starbucks. The air-conditioning is too high, so I move outside, though not without misgivings. It's a small town. Won't some people think it inappropriate if they notice Judith Stitzel sunning herself so soon after her loss? I compromise and sit with my back to the road, the sun's warmth blanketing my neck and arms. I remember what my elegant friend Tachan said at the shiva, surprising me with her earthiness: "Take care of yourself. Eat and sleep. Remember, first and foremost, we are animals."

I draft a letter to my granddaughter, Kaya, who adored her Grandpa Bob. They would toast each other with homemade root beer floats, his childhood favorite, now hers.

Dearest Kaya,

Sometimes words don't seem strong enough to hold our feelings. But sometimes they help us shape them. The obituary and article tell us some of the wonderful things Grandpa did in this world. We know there was even more to his story. That more included his deep love for you and his delight in your many talents (including your handstands) and his pride in your wisdom, generosity and beautiful heart. Always know how much he loves you, how much we both love you. Beyond words.

Our son David remarks with guilty relief that he no longer wakes from sleep worrying what news the next phone call will bring. Will I depend on him too much, calling whenever a strong wind frightens me? Whenever I felt confused, uncertain or frightened, I'd ask Bob, "What would a normal person do?" and he always knew. As he recedes from the constraints of his earthly particulars, he becomes more godlike to us. David wonders whether they'll start a religion around him. "What would Bob say?" Would there be schisms? New gospels?

9/7/07   "How are you feeling? Right now?" That's what one of David's friends asked him, looking him straight in the eye, eliciting truth. How am *I* feeling? Amazed that I am not devastated. Instead, I am planning my day. I will buy some pens and a new notebook at Office Depot. Is it because, as Anna says, I've been grieving for months?

David helps me address my "what if" demons. When I asked him if I was wrong to leave Bob alone in the emergency room to get a cup of coffee, he reminded me I had to take care of myself, like on an airplane, putting one's oxygen mask on first. Should I have acknowledged the tear that slipped beneath the cumbersome breathing apparatus? I see myself again, corralling doctors, asking questions, insisting they make him comfortable. Shut up, demons. I was there for him. And for myself. It is possible to do both.

And yet, some days, I imagine that tear expanding above me, holding the pain of the world.

9/9/07   Later today, my son will return to his wife and daughter in Seattle. I make coffee and begin the first week since Bob's death. "Bob's death"—it sounds more like a creature than an event.

9/10/07   Cleaning out a drawer, I come across Bob's anti-snore strips.

Cleaning out the refrigerator, I see the mustard herring from our last trip to IKEA and three different flavors of cream cheese to tempt his failing appetite. The strips, the fish, the cheese, his asterisks on the calendar reminding me when to recycle—all are evidence of our love.

Bob would have had chemotherapy today. He called his treatment "groucho," rejecting the diminutive "chemo" as too intimate and casual.

Dream: I'm living in my grandmother's small apartment. My bed is large and takes up almost the entire room, but if I look out the high window above the bed, I have an incredible view of the skyline and the Empire State Building. It's not easy to see—you have to stand up and stretch tall—but it's magnificent. From this apartment, I can look across at my parents'. Though the distance is too far for them to see me, they'll know when I open the blinds in the morning that I am well.

9/12/07   A week after David's return to Seattle, his partner Laurel came to be with me. She's a treasure—competent, caring and wise. She's a whiz with Excel and patiently explains how I might use it to manage my finances. I am grateful and overwhelmed.

Several times, imagining her own devastation if she faced a loss like mine, she has broken down, crying. On Friday evening, I sobbed in her arms when she reminded me to light the Sabbath candles. As I assembled the matches, my prayer shawl and the silver candlesticks —a wedding present from my mother and grandmother—I heard Bob's voice. He'd answer my ritual "Good Shabbos," sometimes from another room, sometimes just with the word "Shabbos," as if the "good" were understood, as if he were saying, "I honor your mom and dad and your memory of them. I love you."

In one of our many walks, I confess to Laurel that I regret not attending more to David as a child. I was too young, too self-absorbed, studying for graduate school exams. Bob would counter with his memories, his image of me cradling David as I bathed him; our walks as a family together along the Mississippi, our basset hound trailing.

I don't want to miss the chances my terrible loss allows. I don't want to recover. I want to be true to experiences that are irrevocably mine.

9/16/07   Saying good-bye to Laurel at the airport, hating to let her go, I remark on our nonstop talking the past few days. We imagine Bob's amazed response: "I died. I'm gone. How are you finding so much to talk about?"

My furnace is making its early-season gurgling noises. When I turn the thermostat up, the furnace sounds relieved, as if I finally remembered what to do. It's ready for the new season.

Because they love me and sense my need for company now that both David and Laurel have left, Maggie and Anna invite me to join them in a cabin at Bluestone State Park.

Before I leave, I call friends in Sweden to tell them Bob has died. The year we spent there early in our marriage—and many times afterwards—shaped the rest of our lives. "Bob and Judy. Bob and Judy," repeats Anna-Karin, the wife of Bob's co-worker Pelle. Her grief triggers mine. I feel as if the trip to the state park is a charade. Who do I think I'm kidding, preparing the house for winter, getting the car serviced, packing a suitcase? Big shot! You silly widow. You lonely woman.

One night, wakened from sleep while at the park, I hear Bob calling my name, as if assuring me I still had access to his voice.

One morning, Maggie suggests we each take a different path and record as simply as possible what we noticed.

This morning I followed one sign rather than another and found my way back through a tamped-down road I hadn't used before. Nothing special. A squirrel. Two blue-black butterflies. Trills. Clicks. Chatters. Creatures at work or play. An empty clothesline. Hewn wood near a cabin. Nothing spectacular here. No wind ruffling the leaves. The trees have barely turned. But the light bathes the new-mown grass and grace loosens the knot in my heart. I do not forget the sounds of death or the voices that came before and followed. The tears. The torn fabric across the generations. Not a tragedy here, but a deep sorrow. An ordinary spot. Blue sky. A bench. Some grass. An undistinguished squirrel. More of the same. Nothing more. Enough.

I accompany Maggie and Anna to buy groceries in town. I miss doing errands with Bob, who always made a list to ensure the most efficient driving route. Not a question of time saved, but of elegance, as that word is used in mathematics: the simplest solution. I miss our squabbles. No more fights over what route to take or the appropriate amount of time before slowing down at an intersection, or putting on a turn signal. No more second-guessing. No more guessing at all.

Before I leave Bluestone, Anna looks straight at me and says, "You are a beautiful woman." I decide to believe her. And that handsome motorcyclist at McDonald's on the drive home? What does he see? He wants to know how many miles to Summersville and, happily, I know.

The closer I get to Morgantown, the harder it is to maintain the intermittent illusion that I will see Bob when I get there, that I will wake up—finally—from this ridiculous dream. When I call David on the way home, he tells me he just received a letter from a life insurance company that referred to "the deceased." "It's like one of those cardboard cutouts at a county fair," he says, "where you put your head in another person's costume. How can this possibly have anything to do with me?"

9/23/07   Today I feel I'm doing well. Too well? I don't want to be punished for arrogance.

Still in bed, I hear something fall in the bathroom, but I can't tell what. Is there a ghost? Would it frighten me? How would I make sense of it? I think of writing a play. The ghost is the new life; it's what enters next when you don't close the door.

9/24/07   When I remember events from our earliest days, a fresh grief descends—as if my own past life has been erased. Memories that only Bob treasured mock me. The red kilt I wore on our first date at Yankee Stadium. My watching the elevated trains more carefully than the players on the field. Who will find these slivers amusing? Who will laugh with me?

I join our gardener Mark in our garden, the consummate evidence of Bob's and my love and good fortune. "Two *pishers* from the city," Bob said, the disparaging Yiddish word warding off the evil eye. "Who would have thought?" Out of major reconstruction on our house after the foundation crumbled, we created one-third of an acre of paradise—the "best bed and breakfast in the world," Bob called it. Not without help. Bob's parents' money, as well as ours. A landscaper's planning, as well as our dreams.

Mark says he misses Bob most when he cleans the pond filter, a task Bob enjoyed. No, he says, he doesn't see my loss as comparable to what he would feel if he lost Tina, his dear wife of eight years. "Fifty years," he says, marveling. "You were part of each other. Twins." We talk about plans for next spring's garden. I tell him I'd like the garden neat for October's memorial service. He asks if he needs a suit to attend. Inside the house, he changes a light bulb. Deeper inside, he changes my heart.

9/28/07   Who knew going to the grocery store would release so much pain? I return fifty dollars' worth of useless items—tissues, Icy/Hot, Ensure, Carnation. None of it worked! None of it kept Bob from dying. I bump into things, am sentimental about cereals—instant oatmeal, Wheaties with baseball players on the carton. When will I be hungry again?

As I fold shorts to return to Lands' End, I am thrown back to those brave days of his trying them on before the mirror; together we admired how well they fit over his increasingly small rump. We thought we had more time.

As I move away from Bob's death—four weeks tomorrow—administrative necessities fill my mind. I feel clogged, impatient and judgmental.

I sit by the pond as the Japanese maples deepen in the Western sun. I remember how Bob rescued me from despair when I was struggling with my dissertation; how he carried me joyfully over midlife's threshold for my surprise fiftieth-birthday party in Sweden, how he helped me carry the grief of my parents' deaths two months apart. I'd believe in heaven in a flash if I thought I would see him again.

He was, like me, an atheist, but when people told him they were praying for him, he thanked them warmly. The only person who annoyed him was the volunteer harpist at the cancer center. As soon as he heard a chord rolling down the corridor of the infusion room, he would ask me to close the privacy curtain, as if a mariachi band were on its way, uninvited, to our table.

When I meet with the vice-president of the Health Sciences Center to discuss the memorial the university is organizing, he tells me there are things I don't know about Bob—not secrets, but the details of a life at work. I acknowledge the otherness of this human being who loved me above all others, yet had a separate life, a life in which others knew him differently than I did. I am not jealous. I just wanted more of him as he wanted more of me.

I remember showing him an article I'd seen about a luxurious cross-country train trip. Even if we couldn't fly because of the danger of blood clots, perhaps a train trip would brighten our spirits. But that photo of the smiling man and woman in the romantic train saddened him. He knew we could never be that couple.

October

10/1/07   A marriage license at the beginning and a marriage license at the end. I need one to get social security benefits, but I can't find my copy. I try to stay calm as I write the necessary letter to the Marriage Bureau of the City of New York.

I have to get papers to certify that I am the administrator of Bob's will. I wait in a county office crammed with oversized photos of cheerful dogs, embroidered prayers—"If it can't be easier, Lord, help me to be stronger"—and pink silk flowers. When the clerk returns, I'll be sworn in. I am split between the mourning wife and the efficient executrix.

I talk with David and Laurel about finances; I want to see money management as a way to express my competence and agency—and control. But I feel insecure. How much money can I give to David and Laurel now, rather than waiting until I, too, am dead? Not *can* give, but *want* to give—a heady, empowering distinction. Bob would help me figure it out, though I need him less for fiscal advice than as a moral and emotional compass. We spoke well together about complicated things.

10/2/07   When my nephew Ian calls from Boston to make arrangements to attend Bob's memorial, he's worried about his father, sees significant deterioration. Ivan seems reluctant to plan. Could he afford in-home nursing? At what point would hospice help? Would Ivan even consider it?

My kind family doctor takes the time to ask how I'm doing, when I go for a routine physical. When I ask about a moment Bob's eyes glazed over, he suggests he might have been looking inward, his soul collecting itself for the next stage of the journey. I don't believe in a soul, but I like the sound of the word, and I am strengthened by the doctor's suggestion that because Bob and I engaged deeply with each other for almost fifty years, he was likely part of my brain —physiologically, as well as metaphorically.

When I casually mention to Robert, my strength trainer, that one of Bob's colleagues has arranged to offer up a mass for him, his amazed expression tells me he was imagining a large cathedral, not a small campus chapel. We laugh together. "Dad loved to hear you laugh," Laurel says, when I tell her about the incident. She says she worried she couldn't find the words to describe how much she loved me. But her knowing just when to call me and what to say says everything.

A friend suggests I may be planning too many trips. Another suggests, thinking it a compliment, that the attention Bob is receiving is a reflection of people's affection for me. I resent everyone who thinks they have a better understanding than I do of what's going on.

The happiness that sometimes accompanies my growing competence can drain away in an instant. The jolt of recognition— he's gone forever—reminds me to be cautious. Only when I get home after a pedicure with Joseph do I realize I still have my pants' legs rolled up to my knees. How odd I must have looked at the city hall where I had gone to pick up some death certificates after the appointment. Joseph had said he could teach my husband how to give me a foot massage like the one I was obviously enjoying. The woman next to me suggested I withhold dinner from my husband until he complied. I wanted to say, "My husband's dead." Wouldn't that have sent everyone scurrying to respond! Joseph would have had to translate my words into Vietnamese for the trainee who was learning English: buff, acrylic, French nails, dead.

10/5/07   Preparing for Bob's memorial, I find a file we must have made years
            before. It refers to two songs, "Take Me Out to the Ballgame" and
            "When I Fall in Love," and our favorite Monty Python episode,
            "The Dead Parrot Sketch."

            I balk at writing my signature on the new car insurance form, on
            any document Bob prepared on our behalf. He was in charge of
            those parts of our life, took pride in managing them. I remember
            practicing that signature before we were married, writing *Judith
            Stitzel, Judith Stitzel, Judith Stitzel* all over the margins of my
            college notebooks.

10/6/07   It may have been a mistake to go to my cousin's wedding so soon
            after Bob's death and so many hours away from home, but maybe
            distance didn't matter. As C. S. Lewis laments in *A Grief
            Observed*, "At first I was very afraid of going places where H and
            I had been happy . . . unexpectedly, it makes no difference. . . .
            Her absence is like the sky, spread over everything."

            I wouldn't have described what I felt last night as "fear," without
            C. S. Lewis—"the same fluttering in the stomach, the same restlessness,
            the yawning." Whatever I call it, it was profound, devastating and
            humbling. It began back in my room after the rehearsal dinner,
            when I wanted to call Bob, to give myself some ease before I slept.
            But when I imagined our phone ringing at home, with no one
            there, I collapsed on the hotel bed in tears, kicking my feet like a
            child. Where did he go? Where is he? Bob, where are you?

I glance over at the photo of Bob I carry with me. How will I sleep? How will I rest? How will I do anything if I cannot speak with him tonight? I call David. He is at Kaya's soccer game and leaves the stadium to hear me better. How long did I cry? Who could believe so much mucous? So many secretions? What do they accomplish?

Sometime during the last year, someone said, "You're doing better with Bob's cancer than you did with the Iraq war." Not now! I don't give a shit about the war. Let it rage on. Give me my husband back.

In the hotel coffee shop, I overhear several women planning a memorial. "That's what kills me," one says at least four times. They're talking about another woman preventing them from implementing a great idea. How foolish they are! How foolish we all are, assuring ourselves that we are doing something just a little bit better than the next person.

On the way home from the wedding, the couple who kindly drove me there squabble. *Narishkeit*—the disparaging Yiddish word for foolishness—speaks itself in my head. I am jealous. I miss the self-congratulatory comparisons Bob and I might have enjoyed: "We'd never fight about anything so silly. Aren't we wise? Aren't we special?"

10/9/07   I want to run the film backwards. I want a do-over. I do not say, "I can't go on," because I am going on. But who is the *I* that goes on without steady ground beneath her?

10/10/07   On the way to the Pittsburgh airport to visit my brother in Boston—
my first plane trip since Bob's death—I listen to an audiotape
about writing and am grateful once again for Bob's eager support
when I went back to school for my MFA after I retired. Bob never
tired of proudly telling friends and colleagues that he was married
to a "coed."

As the plane rolls to its berth in a cloudy Boston, I think of those
I've lost:

The world empties, dear brother.
So many are gone,
our mother, our father,
your wife, my husband.
Our parents, underground; Vera, ash;
my sweet man awaiting a student's knife.

I imagine Bob's body as a cadaver.

"He looked just like my father," Bob had told David, describing his
first dissection. "It was quite a shock." Well, let me tell you, Bob,
it's quite a shock to have you gone, despite the fifteen months of
knowing what was coming.

Will he be valued in death, as in life, for traits peculiar to him? I
want more particulars. What do they do with the blood? The
brain? What happened to my brain those last hours I was with him,
knowing and not knowing what was happening? Was he sitting
up when I looked over at his living face for the last time, his eyes
startled and filmy? "He's dying, isn't he?" Is that when they
called the code? What am I trying to retrieve through this
painful excavation?

In Boston, I read the novel my brother Ivan has been working on. All my life, his genius and his sorrow have unarmed me, his alcoholism warring with his accomplishments, my adulation with my insecurity. Fully grown, I'm still hungry for his affection and regard, as if we were brother and nine-years-younger sister at the beginning of our unscripted lives.

Ivan always made me laugh harder than anyone else could. Looking to him for comfort, I explain how unmoored I am by my new responsibilities. Am I paying too much for water? Do I have too many TV channels? "Fuck the water bill and keep the channels," he advises.

10/12/07   Ivan is too sick to talk about Bob at any length. He has a lot of pain this morning. In his lungs. In his back. In his hands, which he tries to warm by moving them over the stove's lit burners, the sleeves of his tattered robe hanging down perilously. It had never occurred to me that my brother would outlive my husband, who was five years younger. I'm assuming I'll outlive my brother. But who knows? I have two planes tomorrow, many streets to cross, terrorist sleeper cells at any time awakening.

I tell my grandniece Gaby that I'll be seeing her when she comes to Morgantown for Bob's memorial. But I want to be with him, not memorializing him. C. S. Lewis warns against remaking the beloved in the image of the survivor's need, smoothing out the wrinkles, instead of respecting them. Fuck memory. I want the Bob who would hate my saying, "Fuck memory," who would hate my saying "fuck" under any circumstances. Usually I restrained myself, in deference to him. Sometimes I didn't. I want to rub up against him, as tender, recalcitrant and refreshing as any body ever was. Before Bob died, I wanted his body, dead or alive, grounding me. Now I realize that it was not the solidity of flesh I desired, but the ballast of his otherness.

On my way home, the plane banks on its ascent from the stopover in New York, and I salute the city of my birth—the city of my parents (gone), where I married my husband (gone)—as it disappears behind me. I think about mothers and fathers who've lost their children to accident, or illness, or war, redeeming their lives through dedication to—even creation of—a cause. Then I imagine retreating to a cloistered life. Soon after arriving home, I dream I'm bleeding from my right side. I've scratched an old wound open, and I'm aware this condition is dangerous.

I decide not to cancel a writer's conference in Iowa at the beginning of November that I scheduled before Bob died. I'll be meeting people who will not know me as Bob's wife, which makes me feel guilty, as if I were being unfaithful. And if I met someone in Iowa and had a quick fling? What a peculiar idea! What old-fashioned language!

10/19/07   The invitations to Bob's memorial have gone out. They look nice. Simple. What the hell do they have to do with me?

Loneliness returns on the shirttails of the daily: hearing old songs on the radio, doing a wash, seeing the small towel Bob used to dry his hair, how he hung it close by the shower door to get at easily. Sometimes I mourn as Bob—not *for* him, but *with* him, as he must have mourned what he was about to lose. This slipping into his no-longer skin is harder to bear than my own grief.

I haven't made the bed since he died. It was our morning ritual, standing within clear sight of each other at the start of our day.

10/21/07 I've been nauseated lately and dizzy, but I "throw myself out of the house"—that's how I've begun to describe the technique to others—and take a walk in the university arboretum. The day shines with promise. Will there still be glorious fall color when guests arrive for the memorial? Pema Chödrön and my other Buddhist teachers tell me impermanence is one of the three truths of the dharma. But for the moment, sorrow's shadow rolls down and the Buddha's wisdom chills my blood. Can it be possible that some day I will label even the unfathomable grief I've been experiencing as just "thinking," a temporary blocking of the free-flow of the breath?

After my walk, I told my friend Loana that I felt a sense of duty to the beauty of the yellow wildflowers. She told me they're called "sulfurs." She said my response went beyond duty, beyond ethics, beyond survivor's guilt: "Nature brings the flame back up because we're part of it. It's beautiful. It doesn't have to be, but it is."

I went to a poetry reading that bored me. No matter. I parallel parked the car! Sure, it was a huge space and still gave me more trouble than it should have. But I tried. I succeeded. I went out at night, in the dark, in the car, and parked it on my own.

10/26/07 So many people are helping me. University staff for the formal service at the medical center, friends for the reception at our home afterwards. I stare at the paper cups and plates being put out to welcome out-of-town guests. Bob's college buddies are coming from around the country to honor him, some bringing real bagels from New York.

I want to be with Bob, watching from afar, hearing him praised and loved. I don't want to be doing well, or badly; don't want to be strong, or weak. I want to be paying attention, not attracting it. I am a cavern of want and refusals. I want to disappear.

10/29/07	Kaya spoke at Bob's memorial, and no one moved me more. She quoted Maya Angelou to describe him: "I've learned that people will forget what you said, people will forget what you did, but people will never forget how you made them feel."

David and I attended an additional ceremony to honor Bob at the Center for Black Culture and Research. The director told David that Bob especially supported students who were having trouble but worked hard and then strove to deserve his trust. David said that was how he remembered growing up—"being affirmed and living up to the confidence."

"I feel like I'm killing him all over again." I couldn't believe my own words. But I know I said them, because Maggie and Anna were standing next to me, in my bedroom, where I was hiding from the guests I had invited for a Sunday farewell brunch. "Enough already!" That's what I was feeling. Maggie and Anna suggested we take a walk in the arboretum after everyone else had gone.

10/30/07	For the past few hours, all I have wanted to do was stay in bed and hide—maybe visiting Nancy and attending that writing conference in Iowa wasn't such a good idea—but the clouds have begun to dissipate. Though tasks nip at my heels now that the memorial is over, there's time to do them when I return. I ask myself one more set of questions: Is there anything that won't wait? If I don't go, am I missing an opportunity to connect to my future self? Would I return better able to deal with worlds inside and out?

In the end, I decide I'll be closer to Bob—and myself —in the clean air of Iowa than in a house heavy with post-memorial grief.

10/31/07   Ivan tries to call me on his cell phone, but he bungles it and I'm
            scared. Could he have fainted? He sounded very tired. He doesn't
            think he taught well. The students were kind. One of them helped
            him get his coat off when he was in too much pain to do it on his
            own. He was going to get stronger meds later this morning. What
            should I cook for him when I visit in December? Will he live
            until then?

            A-Rod has left the Yankees. Someone else was chosen over
            Mattingly. Torre will manage the Dodgers. Nothing's right in
            the world.

November

every once in a while. You itch. You scratch.
Itch again, maybe, in the same place, or nearby.
Scratch again, while you continue to "entertain" others.
you were doing, watching TV perhaps, reading a
cup of coffee. All this was
no more troublesome than a
cough or cramp, every annoying.
But then, even before
they disappear, the

I was cool & take the coming toward
with fingers of its own. Before long
Welts ran or my Flesh
I was my Mirror
had revealed

I played or
I could you crazy & urgents for adjustment
& my growth. I true ominous
involvements, collages & vitamins. A night
or two would pass without
only to be followed by

11/1/07   Next stop Cedar Rapids. I feel more energized as the day goes on. I'm writing in my journal. First lines. Ideas for stories and comic schticks. I'm imagining Bob home when I get home. Not waiting. But available. Amused.

At the conference, when a speaker referred to the birth of her son, I remembered David's birth and saw the momentary fear on Bob's face when the doctor looked shocked. Was something the matter? No, it was David's record-breaking initial urination. It was 1964 and fathers weren't routinely present. But Bob was loving us from the other side of a window. It's not as much fun now to tell that story. Or the one about our gorgeous garden emerging from the chaos of reconstruction. Not as much fun, even with the freedom to embellish and not be interrupted by a mate's inevitable corrections and amendments.

I consider the pleasures of the single life, the assertions of taste that were (often willingly) muted before. Now I can buy a painting that is more abstract than Bob would have liked and hang it anywhere. Our rule as a couple was that, except for our offices, we bought a piece of art only if we both liked it. Yet, whatever we bought and wherever we hung it, Bob knew how to get that nail exactly where I wanted it.

And sometimes when I miss Bob, I know I am mourning my own lost youth, and dread my own demise. That literary word feels right here. The feeling is not nausea exactly, more the prelude to a child's giggle or the moment when sobs threaten to escalate and take our breath away. It's a child's loss I'm remembering, her longing even before words can tame it.

"It's okay," Bob told his mother Betty when he spoke to her moments before she died. "You've done your job. I'm doing well. David and Laurel are happy together. You can let go now if you want to." He told me he could hear her relax into her final breath. She had already picked out her navy bouclé dress. She had already warned us not to bury her with the good pearls. She was ready.

If Bob had been ready, would it have felt any different for me? I have not asked that question before this moment. David and Laurel and I were sure that he would have hated what came next: further weakness, less and less hope, pain. All true. But we never allowed that however rotten he may have felt, he may not have been ready.

11/6/07   It's a gorgeous morning in Iowa: the wind quiet, the morning light fabulous, reddening the still-leaved trees. Some trees, already bare, look like stands of wild grass. After the conference, Nancy took me shopping at Coldwater Creek. The saleslady admired how well I looked in size 10 pants. She thought even the size 8 looked good. She says she can't believe I don't like to wear heels, and I imagine her imagining me as I cut a swath through a room.

11/7/07   It's two months since Bob died and, still, I can't throw his medication away. Like snowflakes in a glass ball, they belonged to a world where will and hope seemed a match for the impossible. And though, with stomach cancer, we never had a chance, I feel tender toward them. I liked counting them out, getting the bottles from the kitchen shelf, my fingers maneuvering expertly among the containers that share homely space with water glasses and jelly jars and spices.

11/14/07   I thought I'd turned a corner after Iowa, even looked forward to a meeting with an accountant, stepping into new territory. But the morning of my meeting, I woke sighing and belching, as I remember my mom doing when she was upset. I almost had an accident driving there, cutting a car off at the exit ramp.

11/15/07   At the Charlotte airport, waiting to change planes to be with David and Laurel for Thanksgiving, I get a call from Ian. His father is in the hospital. He says he's relieved, feels more useful than before. At least he can feed the cats. Will Ivan still be in the hospital in December, when I plan to visit again? Should I go to him now? Could I do so and sustain my own equilibrium?

There's a crisply outlined quarter moon visible from the plane. I remember my mother's pleasure at my precocity when I asked, "Is there a penny moon?" How many moons ago was that? Tonight, the moon is cradled by its more mysterious shadow, earthshine a shade barely lighter than the sky, just enough to reassure us of the fullness to come. Later when I look out, I see only the moon-tip, descending beneath a cloud, like a child's drawing of a sail. As we draw close to Seattle, I feel for a moment that I can, in fact, carry Bob forward with me, not the dying Bob, not the impossibly dead Bob, but the living spirit of our married lives.

11/17/07   David and Laurel help me with bank statements I don't understand. I am grateful for their patience and pedagogical prowess.

Some barely controllable itching that began last summer has returned. I'm less worried than I was, having had some tests to rule out the unlikely, but not impossible, cancer it might reveal. I recall Bob's uncanny ability not to have to scratch an itch. He considered my inability a character flaw, a minor one to be sure, though it allowed him a harmless superiority.

Sometimes I feel I need to rescue memories, like Bob's pleasure in the bright orange dress I bought on Maui. But he needs my help. Through language, laughter—even good works—it is my responsibility to keep us alive.

During a phone call to Ian, in which he sounds exhausted, I offered to come earlier than I intended. I could fly from Seattle to Boston on Jet Blue, return to Seattle and reschedule my frequent flyer trip to Morgantown. I'm pleased with my resourcefulness. Laurel points out wisely that whatever choice I make may leave me wishing I had made the other.

David and I walked around the peninsula at Seward Park, past old-growth forest, past the path on which he walked with his dog Roscoe the last day of Roscoe's life. David was certain we walked this path before with Bob and thrown sticks from the black sand beach across from Mercer Island. But I have no memory of it, and I don't know which is worse, having lost a memory or the chance to make a new one. Grief leaches my confidence, assailing past and future both.

11/20/07   I enjoyed being around the ritual morning sounds of my son's
            house: tooth-brushing, alarm clocks, people shuffling through
            rooms and papers, getting ready for the day. When Kaya greeted
            my cheery "good morning" with a pre-teen's dismissive wave, I
            didn't let it disturb me. But it confirmed my general unsuitability
            as a parent for a modern teenager. I would never be calm enough.
            I'd insist she not say "suck" as often as she did and that she be more
            specific in her complaints. I'd be a pain in the neck.

            Ian called to say that Ivan had checked himself out of the hospital
            without the doctor's okay and wasn't doing at all well at home. I
            booked a red-eye flight on Jet Blue. That felt right. It still feels
            right. So what's the problem?

11/21/07   David hasn't been feeling well and is trying to schedule an ultra-
            sound; he's having trouble swallowing. Could he have pancreatic
            cancer? That's what Bob's mother died of. Too much. Too much.
            Even Laurel seems nervous.

            At times, illogically, I wish my brother dead, instead of my husband.
            After all, he was older, drank for many years, smoked too much,
            refused early treatment for his prostate cancer. There was ample
            evidence that my husband deserved to be alive.

11/22/07   I thought I could take that red-eye flight. But I couldn't. Last
            night, after talking with Ian on the phone, I had a breakdown. I
            understand now why they call it that. The sobs didn't last long. I
            can't even remember what triggered them or what I said to David
            and Laurel when I got off the phone. But I knew that I could not
            healthily be with Ian and Ivan at this time. Not without going
            home first to get my bearings.

When I called Ian to tell him I couldn't come, he said he was not surprised.

When I called Ivan and said, "I'm not as strong as I thought I was," he said, "Neither am I." When I hung up, I broke down again. I wish those sobs had been recorded, so I could hear my grief. How bizarre to need proof of my own sorrow! Why don't I feel entitled to its full measure?

We were ten adults and five children at Thanksgiving dinner. The rooms were warm with good spirits, great food, beautiful decorations, sticks of butter studded with cranberries, an arrangement of pomegranates, kale, and pumpkins. Nasturtium petals in the carrot-orange soup. Those who knew Bob told stories about him, and we brought him into the room for a toast.

I told the story of our first argument as a married couple. I don't remember what it was about, only that he stomped out, saying he was going to get a haircut, and came back almost immediately, already laughing. It was Monday. The barbershop was closed.

11/23/07   Dream: Bob and I are walking in an unfamiliar city where we find a baseball diamond. It's a practice field, but a very famous player is there whom I convince Bob to hang out with. Then I take a walk around the neighborhood. A number of small plots along the sidewalk look like they need some tending, and as I start to pull weeds, I realize this is not my property and that I won't see the fruits of my work. It's not that I begrudge working on another's behalf or that my work won't be acknowledged (although that is part of it), but that I could be using the time to get to know this new place better.

11/26/07   If I were going home to Bob, everything would be fine. This is not a vague yearning, but a precise description of the way I feel. All the stress, strain and uncertainty of the last ten days—David's scare (still unresolved), Ivan's struggle, Ian's struggle—would be manageable if I were going home to my life, to the regularity of its demands and offerings. My bed. My kitchen. My garbage night. My husband.

At the airport food court, I share a table with a man and woman my age who are discussing something they find annoying about Starbucks' system of ordering. She smiles when he brings their coffee to the table. She scrunches up her face when he shows her the gingerbread cookie peeking out of the snowflaked paper bag. "I thought we weren't going to eat any more sweets," she says. How I miss those sweet recriminations.

A friend warns me against getting over-involved with my brother's dying: "This was coming. You knew it. You have your more immediate grief to consider." She doesn't understand that it's not the deaths themselves, but the craters they leave behind, the diminishment when those who carried you close to their hearts leave you behind.

11/28/07   *Re: Cremated Remains of Robert Stitzel*

Dear Judith,

We are writing to inform you that the cremated remains of, **Robert Stitzel**, *are ready to be returned to you. Please call to verify your mailing address and telephone number, and provide us with a date to send them. You can call the Human Gift Registry Monday through Friday between the hours of 8:15 am – 4:45 p.m.*

Again, we wish to extend our sincere appreciation for the loving and generous gift that your loved one has given for the advancement of medical science and research.

If you have any questions, please let us know.

Sincerely yours,

Human Gift Registry

I stomped around the kitchen, not believing what I had just read. First, there's the timing. Couldn't they have waited until the turkey was digested? And then: "Re: Cremated Remains of Robert Stitzel." Was this an order for envelopes? And those commas before and after Bob's name? No. Those aren't commas at all, but placeholders to indicate where in a mass-produced letter the name of the deceased—any fuckin' deceased—will appear in BOLD. And are they really planning to mail the ashes to me? Wrapped for the holiday?

I knew there'd be a ceremony to honor donors sometime during the year, and I assumed I'd pick up the ashes at that time when I might have more fully absorbed the impossible reality of his being gone. I never dreamt of such an insulting institutional intrusion.

And how could they use him up so soon? Was his body not as useful as they had hoped? I thought he'd be around for a while, perhaps taken out often to demonstrate something, perhaps loved again by some sweet youth who saw in him a kind face.

11/30/07   I've taken a late afternoon break at Starbucks, allowed a caramel macchiato and the convincingly cheerful treatment of the barista to soothe me. Some day I will inhabit a world where Bob's absence no longer pulls at my heart and wholeness. Today, that admission carries grief in its arms.

Outside, the evening falls beyond black pines precise against the rose insistence of sky. Slowly, color drains from the gray stripes, and purple replaces red. Edges blur and trees give up their egos, disappearing into sky. A final moment of pink effulgence, easily missed, as when a lover turns too late to wave goodbye.

December

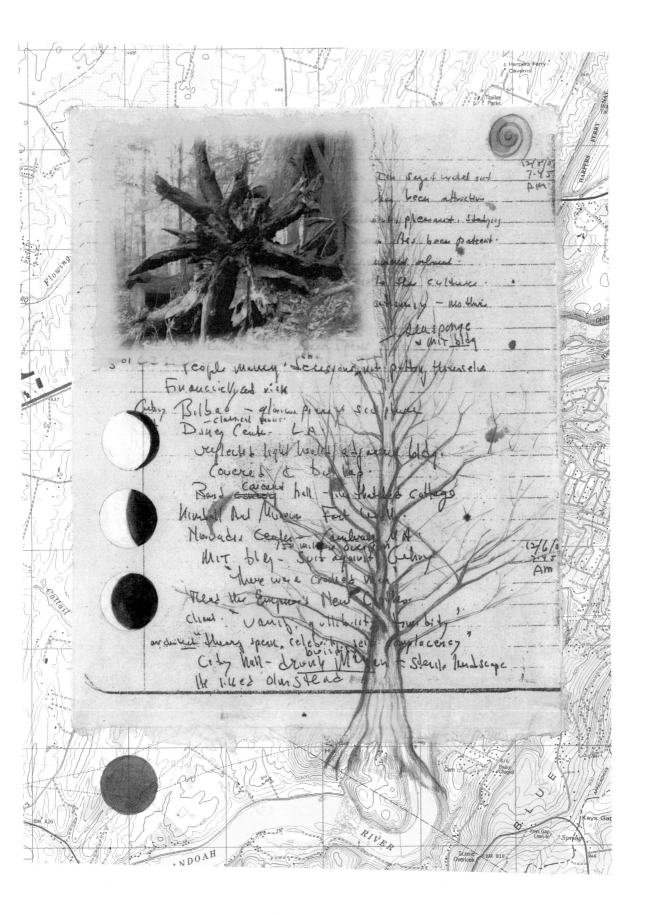

12/2/07   When I do get to Boston, Ivan is hospitalized again. I'm in his apartment, where I've visited so many times, with our parents, with Bob, but now there are only Ivan's cats. I don't like these cats. Had Ché stayed on my bed longer last night, had any of them come to me for comfort, I might have felt differently. But they did not extend themselves. Too bad. Too sad. Too . . . cat.

How long should I stay? What do I have the strength for? If I were still caring for Bob, I might not have been able to come at all. Ian and Ivan would have done as well as they could and neither would have expected more of me (or me, more of myself).

12/6/07   I visit nursing homes with Ian and help Ivan read his students' final papers and get them graded. I stay at my brother's side for hours, pampering him, arranging pillows, talking with nurses on his behalf. "Judy Stitzel," he says, his voice soft with gratitude and without a tinge of his usual irony, "when did you become a saint?"

This afternoon, I am so tired, I nap on a couch in the hospital hallway, using my backpack as a pillow. I offer to return later in the month to give Ian and Maria a break over the holidays, but I know, for now, I need the shelter of my own home.

12/9/07   Back in Morgantown, I try to regain my balance. I remind myself that, for the moment, I am in charge of my time and space and privacy, answering to no one, responsible for no one, refusing interruptions. But there are signals of instability. Last night, I behaved like a crazy woman at Panera's, insisting that since I waited so long for my food, they should give me a discount. When I was offered a free coffee instead, I refused, then accepted, then apologized. Oh my! When I told Maggie about the incident, she suggested gently that I consider seeing a counselor.

Drifting off to sleep, I imagine writing a musical about writing a musical about a nursing home. I imagine the sick person in the middle of the stage during the entire play, with nurses, doctors, visitors walking in and out, alternatively taking charge. I like the idea of the play being about the writing more than about the nursing home.

12/13/07   I force myself to open a bill from the hospital. Thank God the $27,000 they mistakenly charged and I have been fighting to get removed was finally gone. But now what? What will I do with the energy I've been stoking for further battles with the billing office and the insurance company? My triumph means shit if I can't get Bob back. Sure, I can tell my tales of woes and accomplishment to Maggie and Anna, or Sharon and Irv, or David and Laurel, but that's not the same as telling someone who knows what you've been through and whose attentiveness stretches as far as his love.

12/15/07   I water the houseplants and acknowledge the comfort of kitchen heat. I open the living room curtains all the way and think about washing them. I fill the bird feeder. I feel that if I let go of certain things—Bob's old socks, maybe—it will be easier to incorporate what is permanent about our years together, the love, the travels, what is ours in this home. I admire our Australian paintings by two indigenous women. There was never any question that we would buy both of them.

Reading Pema Chödrön about compassion and *tonglen* helps. Breathing in pain and breathing out relief, I connect with a feeling I can't always sustain of assuming that people are doing the best they can under their circumstances—the manager at Panera's, the guy who wrote the letter about Bob's ashes, whoever wrote a fund-raising letter for the hospital addressed to former patients, not realizing they might be dead.

12/17/07   Leaving a holiday party early because I was afraid of driving in the snow, I let my body remember how Bob took the turns—steady pressure, some speed. When I told David how unexpectedly secure I felt, he said, "Bob was your copilot."

Agnes and Paul, the couple who clean my house, visit with tangerines and cake and leave me with energy to respond to some of the letters I still receive three months after Bob died.

12/18/07   Today Ivan will be moved from the rehab hospital to a nursing home, though not the one Ian and I liked most, which didn't have a vacancy. I'm going to Boston again next week. When I told my doctor how tired I was, he calmly remarked that my grief had reached flood stage and prescribed some anti-anxiety pills to take on my trip.

| 12/20/07 | I've picked up Bob's ashes. A friend and social worker suggests I might want to keep some of them in a vial and wear it as a necklace. That gives me the creeps. Is that why I say, somewhat provocatively, "I don't think I'd want him to see everything I do"? |

I've picked up Bob's ashes. A friend and social worker suggests I might want to keep some of them in a vial and wear it as a necklace. That gives me the creeps. Is that why I say, somewhat provocatively, "I don't think I'd want him to see everything I do"?

In Pema Chödrön's *The Wisdom of No Escape* I read, "Maybe you're scared of the most exciting things you have yet to learn." She reminds me that Alice in Wonderland didn't "grab for the edges... She just fell and looked at things as she went down. Then when she landed, she was in a new place."

12/21/07

This morning, I found a renewal request for *Sports Collectors' Digest*. I write a note: "With great sadness I must tell you that my husband, for many years a loyal reader, has died." It shouldn't be so easy to cancel a man's subscriptions.

I am getting ready for a holiday season without Bob. The present collapses into a disappearing past, like the spaces between the ribs of an accordion. I turn down an invitation to a large Christmas party. Some people find comfort in knowing that what they're feeling others have felt—the implied promise that, believe it or not, eventually they, too, will be fine. But I am offended by that assurance of similarity. I prefer my singularity and do not want to squander my grief in conversation.

Sitting at the table, making out a check to a friend, I wonder whether to order a new checkbook. I yearn for the lovely division of power and worry, the caretaking, the gentle annoyances and feelings of competence on both sides, the routine, the predictability, the twoness of it all.

Looking out the patio door at our garden below, I imagine Bob lovingly pruning the pyracantha.

12/23/07   I answer my cell phone on the way to the Pittsburgh airport. "Ivan died this morning," Ian tells me. The situation got much worse, very quickly. There may have been negligence. He feels he should have been at the hospital by his father's side. I recall the sense of failure the night Bob died—"I tried so hard"—and offer my words to Ian, hoping they will acknowledge—and then drain—the disabling guilt of impotence.

Later, as I approach the boarding area, I hear the familiar warning: "Caution. Moving steps are coming to an end. Please attend to children and watch your step. Thank you."

Although it stinks of cat feces and hasn't been cleaned since I was here, I still choose to stay in my brother's apartment rather than a hotel room. I'll clean it in the morning. Ché seems to know Ivan is dead. He leans against me as I write, nudging my arm. For a while I indulge him, then push him away, frightened by my roughness. But he comes back, and I am more gentle.

Ian and I grow more and more uneasy as days pass; we are reminders to each other of what we didn't—couldn't—do.

12/25/07   My grandniece Gaby asks why people die. Ian and Maria tell her it happens when people are very sick or old. "Do children ever die?" she asks. They say it's rare. She's still not satisfied. "Do children grow old?" she wants to know. "No," Ian says, and then adds, "once they're old, they're no longer children." I wonder if she's comforted.

12/26/07   Sitting at Ivan's table, littered with the cruel reminders of disorderly days, I leaf through pages of his unfinished manuscripts. What will David and Laurel find upon my death?

What is my responsibility to the dead? To the living? To myself? To the world? Now that Ivan's dead, I can write anything at all, or nothing. I'm reacting as if his life had something to do with my writing or not writing to begin with, which it did, but for how long can I ride on that excuse?

12/27/07   Gaby is annoyed when Maria says Ivan would be proud of her. "But he's dead!" she says. I approve of her refusal to be comforted. I get annoyed when people invoke presumptions about the dead to comment on the behavior of the living.

I accompany Ian to get some questions answered about Ivan's cremation, but he and Maria will attend alone. I visit the public library where there is an exhibit of William Steig's life and work. I note his wife's comments on a caption in a display case: "He was a tragicomic artist, surely a difficult thing to be. You have to feel both the truth and the grief of the truth and find a way to present them with redeeming delight."

12/28/07   Sudden chest pain. Too much coffee? Heart attack? Anxiety? Take a pill?

I think I should be doing more to get the word out about Ivan's death, write an appropriate obituary for the *Boston Globe*, try to get one in *The New York Times*. Or should Ian be doing more? Or are both of us doing the best we can? Ian is getting tired of my suggestions.

I need Bob's equanimity. He could always flatten out the protuberant molehills, remind me of the actual elevation, and bring me back to earth. He might suggest we watch Monty Python "climbing" the north face of the Uxbridge Road.

January

...not be easily tired by ... new & beloved
... or ...

... ---though ... felt ... I never channeling --
His reading Sparrow's ... ... An Absent Parent.
The Sun, Feb 2008, 3/6 ... by ...
Then I read three poems ... ...
... away from beginning to end.
1/25/06 ... ... junk dealer
1/30 DEVON from NY- NY on PENN JOURNAL
2/5/06 "Baby Bob Bob Do you not think ...
6:09PM ... can't you help me?
       ... Can't you come. Look you ...
       I'm on an upstairs deck. We're visiting
       ... maybe ... More there at least
       one child. They ask me for the air-- that
       I am pretty ... it is "pretty." I think
       that's when ... I've gotten my
       foot stuck under a piece of ... I
       keep playing at loose pickets & now
       I can't get my foot out- I'm ...
       I'll break it or hurt myself. ...
       standing close to the wall. ...
       I think he must be seeing
       me) As I awoke, calling out ...
       dream. I realize he may not ...
       something has happened.

1/3/08   Back home in West Virginia. A day stretches ahead of me. What
           will I do? Write in my journal? Answer letters? Pay bills. My only
           anchor is Robert, my trainer, at 3:30. I decide to read in bed, with
           a tangerine, cold coffee, a mint and Claudia Rankine's *Don't Let
           Me Be Lonely*, which I bought while in Boston. Her definition of
           loneliness is accurate: "What we can't do for each other."

1/5/08   It's taken some doing, but I got good flights to New York for the
           Association of Writers and Writing Programs conference and to
           Florida to see Micki. I'm proud of myself, despite people telling me
           I'm traveling too much. But now I want to follow all this talented
           organizing by just hanging out with Bob.

1/6/08   How polite must we be to those who fail to comfort us?

           They mean well when they tell us about their own husbands
           and wives, their cats and dogs and, yes, their parrots and broken
           appliances.

           A friend says: "You'll have your memories."

           Another says: "At least he's not suffering."

           And then someone adds, "I hope next year is better."

           How can it be better? My husband won't die, that's true. But he'll
           be dead for the whole year. Please—unless you can rewind the
           spool—keep your sympathy to yourself!

| 1/7/08 | I bump along successfully on the surface while fissures threaten underneath. Like icebergs, I am dangerous. A friend annoys me by being too analytical in discussing a dispute with a neighbor. "You could die tomorrow," I say. "Do you want to spend your last day thinking about property lines?" The next day I call to apologize. |

| 1/9/08 | Finally, I get myself to a counselor. |

During our first session, I told Stephanie about Bob's "good death," compared to my brother's. I told her about Bob's modest desires, his gratitude, his only wanting "more of the same" and not getting it. "Not continuing to get it," she corrected me. I told her how much he loved his work, his home, his garden, his son and granddaughter. "And you," she added.

Bob loved my neck. Would he have loved it into my seventies? My eighties?

I like Stephanie, but I wonder if she'll understand how my writing fits into my grieving and my life. I think she values it, but will she identify it, as I do, as an engine towards my future?

| 1/10/08 | In a few days, our son will be forty-four. His first birthday without his father. He shared almost as many years with Bob as I did. I, too, was something of a baby when we met—unformed, and with many needs—but already, I suppose, with qualities he recognized as worthy and desirable. This year I will be singing "Happy Birthday, dear David" alone. |

1/14/08   Claudia, the artist who reintroduced me to Buddhist meditation, called to suggest we work together on a project. We started one in the past, based on a journal I kept about my garden and my weathervane goose. But it didn't catch fire. Perhaps it's time to try again. Something from my current journals, she suggests. I'm pleased.

I yearn for the daily continuity of my life with Bob, the small triumphs he'd bring home when he made a student's life easier. I remember how relieved he was when he dropped out of the race for academic provost. He was getting tired of being asked in the interviews what his "vision" was. He valued people who had vision, admired Jacques Barzun, for instance. But he preferred the daily opportunities to assist students and faculty. When he awoke with a terrible headache the day of the final interview, he called immediately and withdrew his name.

A call from one of his students, Constinia, is an unexpected treat. She had never known a couple whose mutual support was so strong, she said. When I told her how sad I felt when I saw Bob's favorite suede coat hanging in the closet, she knew the coat immediately. "That big brown one, right?" I imagined him in her vision, recognized and alive, and happiness nuzzled my sadness. He had good years with that forty-year-old coat. We had good years with each other in Sweden, where he bought it. In West Virginia, where we lived.

1/15/08   It's visceral and disabling, that freefall when I think I've lost my keys, my credit card, my journal, my confidence.

Sometimes there is a direct channel from a thought to the tear ducts. What's happening then? And music—what is it about music that reaches places where tears lie ready, connecting us to ancient sorrow?

1/17/08   I awoke to snow much heavier than predicted. Will I get to my
           counseling session? I have trouble identifying when I can do
           something on my own, when I can't, and when it's perfectly
           legitimate to reveal vulnerability and ask for help.

           Thanks to a call to Stephanie, I drove to her office despite the
           snow. I backed out of my garage and negotiated the short distance
           to what turned out to be a completely cleared road. She had
           answered all my "what ifs." She reminded me to take my AAA
           card. She asked me to consider how I would feel if I tried and
           succeeded. No, I didn't get out of the driveway in one smooth
           motion as Bob did. But I got out. When I arrived, she applauded.

           Stephanie sees me as someone who has always enjoyed challenges
           and mentions as an example my going back to school for an MFA
           after I retired. I see her point. But sometimes I wonder if Bob kept
           me less confident in certain areas than he might have and if I was
           complicit. She wants to know who I was even before Bob. Who
           indeed? I was sixteen. An "A" student. A loved daughter. A child.

           Unlike people who explored self while they were young and before
           they were partnered, I am only now exploring who I am alone.
           It's as if I'm doing it backwards, so that I will, whenever I die, die
           young. Yet it's painful to realize that I may do things alone that I
           might not have done were we to have lived together to the end.
           And painful to realize Bob will not be at my bedside when I die.

1/18/08   David calls to tell me he isn't sure he'll be able to come to Ivan's
           memorial. He's not been feeling strong physically or emotionally.
           I want him to take care of himself. I want him to be with me. It
           never occurred to me that he wouldn't be.

I told Stephanie about being pregnant with David, about deliberately fighting back a bout of morning sickness when I was on my way to teach a class at the University of Minnesota. I wasn't boasting. I was confessing that I had missed some of the enjoyment, as well as interferences, of expecting a baby by focusing so doggedly on getting my Ph.D. I told her I didn't want to miss anything while grieving for Bob. I had been given a second chance to connect my head and my heart.

1/20/08   At the Martin Luther King Day Awards ceremony, a friend came over to tell me how good it was to see Bob's name on the program as last year's awardee. "He was the bow on the present," she said. Not that he was superfluous or his contribution superficial. She meant that his spirit permeated the atmosphere, made other people better. "Without the bow," she said, "a present is just a package."

Why am I filling up months with travel? Why am I not writing more? I will never have Bob in the flesh again. But why that thought just now? From what source and for what purpose that rush of feeling, throwing me once again into those last two weeks before his death, imagining them from his point of view, praying he didn't feel abandoned, that he wasn't lonely. "Judith, can we go to bed now?"

1/22/08   David will come to the memorial. I am relieved and don't ask what
           helped him to decide. He tells me he wishes he knew more about
           his father's boyhood playing shortstop, wants to know if I've thrown
           away Bob's much-too-small baseball jacket. He says that before his
           father's illness, he felt immortal. So did Bob. I never did.

           I finally told that barista at Starbucks to stop calling me "babe,"
           or "honey," or "cutie." "What should I call you?" he asked. "Just
           Judith, thank you."

           Claudia likes the journal pages I've begun to share with her. She
           says I'm not hiding anything.

1/26/08   I am in a friend's apartment in New York, with a view of the
           Chrysler building within a sliver of unlikely space. The city
           noises—garbage trucks, Con Edison repairs, police and
           fire sirens—comfort me. I know my way around. I am reading
           Thomas Moore's *Care of the Soul.*

1/29/08   When I called Stephanie, she asked how I was handling not being
           able to check in with Bob at the end of the day. I was shocked to
           realize how different things were from my breakdown in Baltimore
           at Deborah's wedding in September.

           Yet it's not all easy. Walking in my old neighborhood, I noticed that
           a crucial landmark has been desecrated and that I won't be able to
           share the news. For years, the lime-green dome of the Most Holy
           Redeemer Church, across from the apartment building I was born
           in, loomed tall enough so that, if we sat on the right side of the
           plane, Bob and I could identify it as we swooped down on

La Guardia Airport. Now that dome was a muddy brown, someone's failed attempt at bronze. "At least Bob never got to see such a terrible thing" is the phrase that knocked at my door and I laughed at the intrusive cliché.

1/31/08   I'm tired of missing Bob.

February

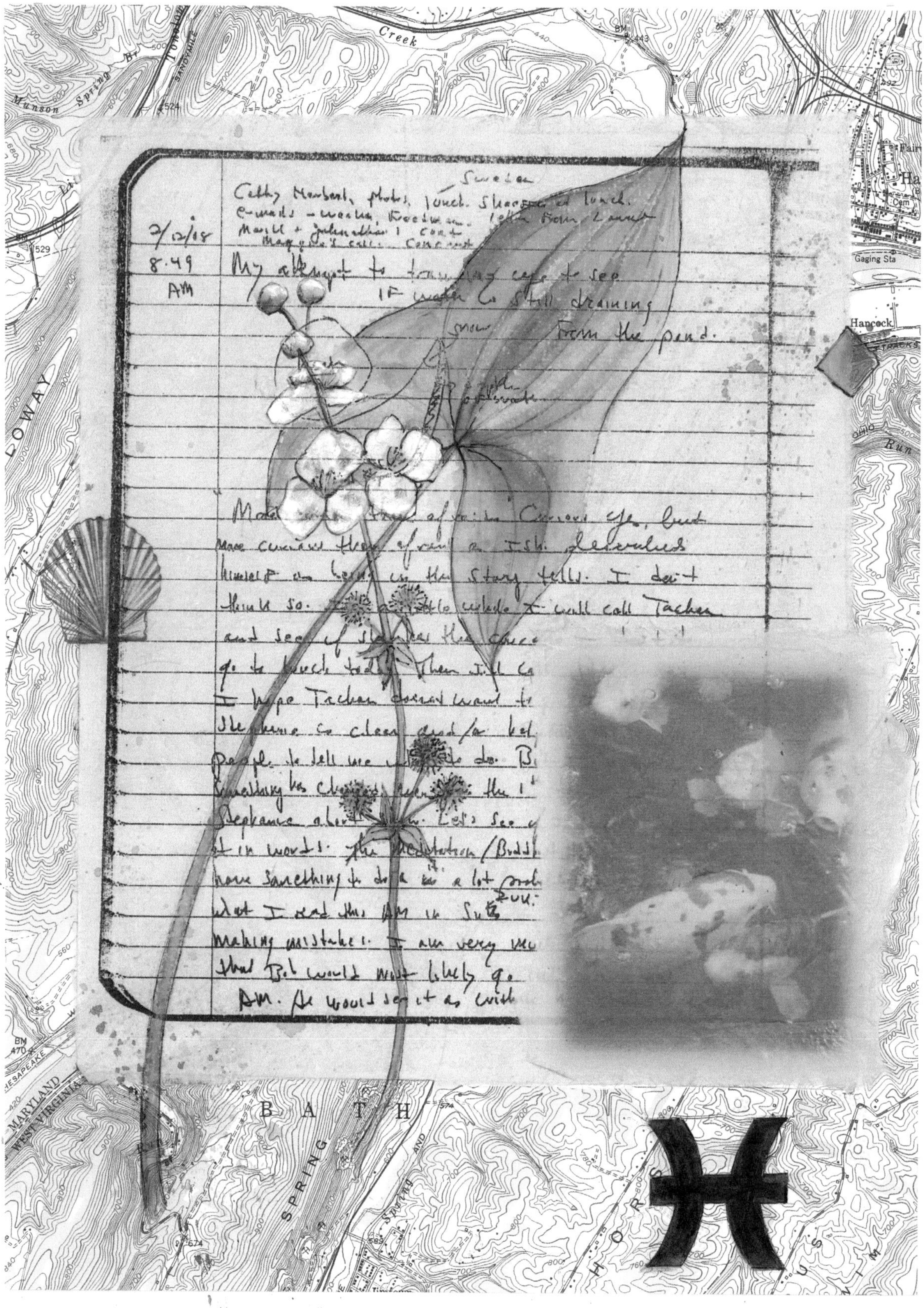
Creek
Munson Spring Br
Gaging Sta
Hancock
Run
MARYLAND
WEST VIRGINIA
B A T H
SPRING
8.49
AM
From the pond.

2/2/08   At the conference, a panelist proclaims that humor writing is
           transgressive, catching the reader in the act of knowing. I like that,
           look forward to my own future writing. But when I walk confidently
           from one session to the next, grief's trapdoor opens and I slip,
           fingers grasping for a hold. I don't want to transgress. I don't want
           to be funny. I want to go home to my husband.

2/4/08   At La Guardia Airport, the bank of phones from which I used to
           call my parents is gone. I loved checking in with them from the
           airport, imagining them in the kitchen, dawdling over coffee, Dad
           finishing the paper, looking for an address among his yellowing
           note cards. Mom might be finishing an article in *The New Yorker*
           or checking the date on a reminder postcard for a museum
           exhibit. Whatever battle between them might have flared during
           the last minutes of our visit would have been forgotten or postponed.
           "How'd you get there so quickly? The cabbie must have driven like
           a maniac," my dad might have said.

           Coming down the escalator into the Pittsburgh baggage claim area,
           I looked for Bob. Coming into the house, I looked for Bob. Hadn't
           I given him plenty of time to come home? When David and I talk
           on the phone later in the afternoon, he tells me he's read a story
           about the dead returning. But there's a hitch. They have their own
           ideas about what to do next, which freaks out their survivors. What
           would freak me out? What would I expect? What might have
           to change?

2/5/08   I'm home. "Now what?" In less than five minutes, I've misplaced my coffee cup twice—first, leaving it on the telephone table, next, on the shelf outside the bathroom. I apologize to the cup for not concentrating on what I am doing. The cup accepts.

The snow is beautiful. I will take time to open the new bag of feed for the birds, the "rabbis of the air," poet Philip Terman calls them.

As I walk between study and kitchen, between bedroom and basement, it occurs to me that I could save time if I set up Bob's study as my financial/business headquarters. At the very least, I need an in-box and an out-box.

I'm glad I went to synagogue last night. I enjoy being in a community of shared experience, singing the songs, accepting the hugs, but I can't ignore that I'm saying things, promising things, asking for things from a God I don't believe in.

2/9/08   Claudia is coming over to discuss our project and I offer to make lunch. Shopping is less fraught than the first time after Bob died. I am happy to be getting grapes, flowers, crackers, and biscotti, happy to be making the house attractive for a guest. On the drive to the store, I listen to Ramsey Lewis, very loud. It's sunny for February and I feel like dancing.

As I come down the driveway into my garage, I remember Bob's footsteps. Whatever he was doing inside, he'd hear the car and come to help me unpack.

Dream: Bob and I are on a wide beach. He's enjoying his time on the blanket, while I walk away over a small rise. From this spot, I realize that the beach is more expansive than we had realized and that it disappears with a sweep into the ocean. I cannot see Bob from this spot, and I consider going back to share what I see. But I'm aware that I won't be able to describe it well enough to convince him to follow me, and so, I will have spoiled things for both of us. I continue on my own and give my body over to a natural sand slide, which moves me along at a thrilling speed. Though I wish again for Bob to be with me, I enter the vast ocean alone.

2/10/08   The wild wind predicted for last night has come this morning. I hear its solitary whoosh and then the rattling sound as it pushes against the outdoor furniture covers. What if they rip? Will I know how to locate new protective coverings? What size would I need? What brand? Where is that catalogue Bob ordered from?

Some shingles off the roof, a garbage can on the far side of the lawn, but the house is basically unscathed. I remember Bob shocking the roofers—how long ago was that?—joking about how many roof-lives he still had. We were immortal then, humor easy on our lips, grief beyond the horizon.

2/12/08   I'm at a familiar place, teetering on the edge of one of those precipices from which it is easy to tumble. Were the door to open now and Bob walk in, I would say, "Thank God. Not a moment too soon. I've done everything I can to live normally and a lot of people have helped me, Bobby shoveling the snow, Mark checking the pond, Sherry inviting me to dinner. But, now, I'm at my wits' end."

I dream about a performance artist who is pretending to cut up a male body. There's no danger. There's no blood. She's laughing at herself. But there's a clear sense of outrage and daring. She is stepping close to a line of decency, if not over it. I am fascinated. In my waking life, I'd been talking about the surprises that come as one learns to live alone, unpartnered, doing things one assumed just got done on their own. But nothing in those conversations suggested the bizarre quality of the dream-woman's performance.

2/13/08   Mark, my gardener, is fully aware how hard the spring will be for me.

2/14/08   I remember Bob arranging to have a barbershop quartet come to the house and sing to me, its paunchy leader giving me one deep-red rose. I was embarrassed at first, then pleased. Other than that, we rarely recognized Valentine's Day—maybe a card, maybe not. But last night, when no one I phoned returned my call, even though I had assured them they didn't have to, I was hurt. It would have been evidence that on this day of commercial sanctioning of love, people stopped whatever else they were doing to make room for me.

A friend asked what I would do once I got over the resistance to scheduling any regular appointments or obligations. I don't think she was being critical, but the word caught my attention. I didn't see it as resistance, but as an affirmation of my need to give myself room to expand and contract as I needed to.

I have prepared materials for the accountant to do my taxes. My taxes. That singular possessive came out before I had a chance to write "our" and correct it. Today, as I did errands at Petco, Walmart,

Lowe's, I anticipated a time, many times, when minutes, hours, days (is it possible?) will go by without my thinking about my husband.

2/18/08   Today begins the week in which I will be alone on Bob's birthday. Not exactly. I'll be with David and Maggie at my brother's memorial. But Bob will not be there. *2/22/37.* Those are the numerals he recited to the cancer center nurses week after week, complying good-naturedly with the requirements to state your birth date every single time you came. Now they are the opening phrase of a completed story: *2/22/37-9/1/07.*

What will be over when this week is over? When I spoke with Loana about the first anniversary of Bob's death approaching, one of us said, "It could be yesterday," and the other replied, "Everything could be yesterday," and we both laughed. Everything will be yesterday. But not everything will be tomorrow.

2/22/08   My mother is much on my mind during the days in Boston. I imagine her after a visit to a museum, or a stylish haircut, having a cup of coffee or soup in a small shop on Madison Avenue, a lovely scarf across her shoulders. Yearning for more than she felt life gave her, but, at that moment, content. I think of my father who, like Bob, could go beyond the needs of self and the infirmities of others to do the best possible in an imperfect world. I worry about how David is going to do without his father. I'm so grateful he felt well enough to be with me at Ivan's memorial.

2/23/08   Dream: Bob and I had been showering together and I was going to wash his hair before we finished, but I had forgotten. So we've gotten dressed, and there he is with wispy hair, looking disappointed. He wasn't going to say anything, but I assured him we could get in the shower again, and I would wash his hair, either at the beginning—so I wouldn't forget—or at the end, so we could look forward to it.

The memorial was perfect, friends coming from around the country and through the generations of Ivan's rich life. Even small flaws were occasions for ingenuity. When the fasteners brought to hold the booklets together were too small, I panicked, until Maggie suggested I need not get involved. Soon someone discovered a solution. Two fasteners in each hole worked just fine.

Toward the end of the post-memorial family brunch, I felt Bob beside me, restless and ready to leave. It was comforting being with family, but he'd had enough talk. Now he wanted to be alone.

"You grew up with them," someone says with heartfelt recognition of my loss—a husband and a brother within two months.

The newspaper says there will be a lunar eclipse tonight. I feel implicated in the eclipse. Odd word, I know, but truthful. Even in an eclipse, a glow remains behind, pulsing in the darkness.

2/26/08   I've scheduled myself so tightly for the next few weeks that I have little time to be alone. Tomorrow I leave for Florida, visit a former student in Orlando, celebrate a friend's 80th birthday in The Villages, then visit with Micki in Key West.

Tumultuous dreams with the same themes—the rewards and dangers of taking risks, the play between curiosity and fear. In one of them a child follows David and me, though neither of us feels responsible for her. She is impish, unpredictable, attractive and disarming. In another, a male version of this girl sends himself rolling down steep hills, hungry for the stream and lushness at the bottom and the huge butterflies that materialize out of one of the banks. How will he climb the slope again? Will it be up to us to wait for him? I'm worried and annoyed. But the beauty, the desire and the butterflies make his actions understandable. He must give himself up to the air.

March

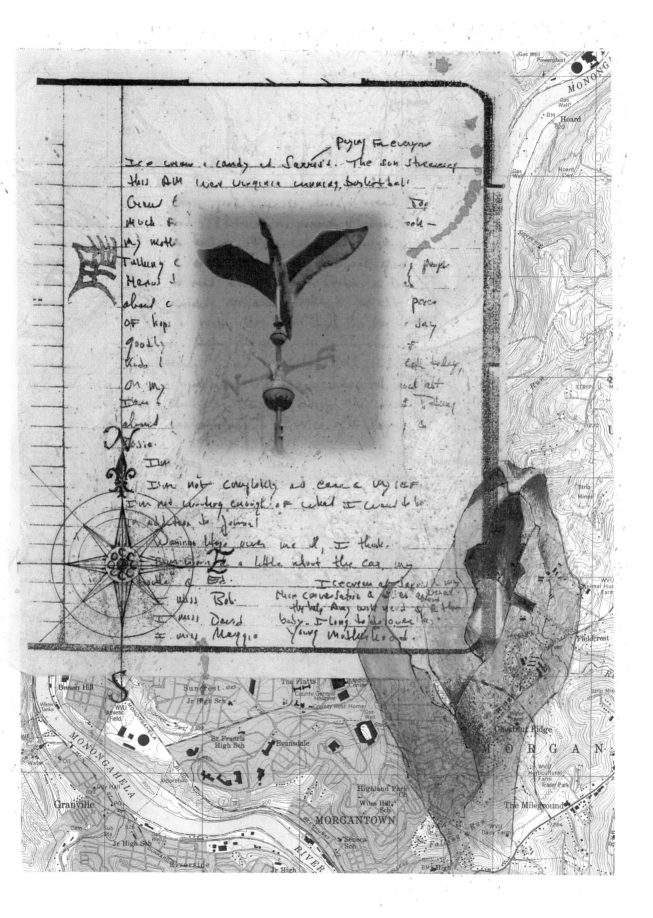

3/10/08   Leaving Key West, I am as sad as I've been since Bob died. It feels like the first sadness, when I grieved more for his losses than for my own, remembering his pleasure in coming home from a long trip, delighted to see our house undamaged, to get the mail and pay bills, to embrace the holiness of our daily life together.

Watching airline ads for Hawaii on the retractable screen in front of my seat, I longed for Bob, for the chance to share memories of our trip with our seven-year-old son to Australia via Hawaii, Fiji and American Samoa. I remember the rainbow swizzle sticks and the waiters singing "Happy Anniversary" to celebrating couples. I miss being able to turn and ask, "What else do you remember?" Our first mahi-mahi (before it became popular)? The dark flesh, the new taste? Remember mai tais? Strawberry daiquiris? It was the beginning of an adventure, the sabbatical ahead of us, everything ahead of us.

I'm the fulcrum of a seesaw, but the sides are dangerously uneven. We never know what we'll remember and what we will not be able to forget.

3/12/08   I've made my first phone call on my new Verizon long-distance plan. Did I make the right choice? Am I paying too much? Bob would not have gotten involved in this phone business. "Do what you want," he would have said with an annoyance I crave. I hate all this freedom.

Since coming home, my grief feels raw, like everything before was a tease or dare. Laurel urges me to be kind to myself, to remember that spring will be a challenge, relentless and unavoidable, plants emerging when they will, without regard for my readiness or desire.

Stephanie helps me speak the sorrows of the season and the terror of my impotence. Bob is not coming back. We talk about John Fowles's *The Collector*, a book that has long terrified me. No matter what approach the kidnapped girl took—compassion, flirtation, rational discussion—nothing worked. In the end, her kidnapper killed her. The worst thing that could happen happened, and she was powerless. "I tried so hard." It wasn't enough.

Yet something is changing. I feel the spaciousness that meditation can provide. "Available" is the word that comes to mind.

On a walk in the arboretum, a muskrat stopped long enough to be seen before sensing me and toddling off, its tail thick with assurance. A biker said hello. A walker passed me silently. I took the Upper Rumsey Trail back to the Guthrie Trail; it was craggier and steeper and a better conclusion for my walk. I could have tripped. But I didn't.

I dream that Bob and I are in the back of a car, perhaps a limo. Our destination is close, so we are not worried. Even though the trip is taking much longer than expected, we can afford the delay. At this realization, I turn towards him and lean down into a kiss. We are both surprised and amused. We laugh out loud, not sure what's funny, but aware that we are in love with and a part of each other.

3/14/08   I feel like a wave has dropped me on *insecure island*, where everything is as it shouldn't be, all opportunities missed and fears enhanced. My brother, the real writer. Me the imposter, the lazy one, unable to go or stay deep enough. Judith, the foolish survivor.

My doubts are very old. What is being offered once again is the challenge of where to place my energies and talents and inclinations. What is most important to me now? What doors do I need to open and close? Should I get new wallpaper? Paper something over? Start fresh? What am I afraid of?

I dream I'm walking around a small lagoon beside a woman who is attracting the swimming birds in an unusual way. She blows at them which, surprisingly, brings them closer, their feathers fluffed by her puff of air. When I describe this technique to someone else, the woman quickly interposes that it took years for her to perfect it and that I shouldn't try. It's clear she's afraid that I would misinterpret her technique, making it look much simpler than it was.

David tells me he's impressed by my ability to look towards a future unshadowed by death. I do not tell him that I'll be ready to be with Bob when the time arrives. I feel this even as I know how many things may intervene between now and then, how many people, even how many loves, however unlikely that now seems.

3/19/08   *Dear Bob,*

*Hi love. I'm worried this morning. I hear you say, "Don't be." Not
because you're discounting my worry, but because you think that one
should act on what is actionable and put the rest to rest. One of your
favorite expressions, "Guilt is a useless emotion," was more Buddhist
than you knew.*

*Should we have spoken more about dying? Did I fail you at the end? I
told you I would stay with you that last night. I feel you heard me. But
before that, did I attend sufficiently to your inner life? You seemed less
concerned than I about roads not taken. You were troubled for a while
when you withdrew from the search for Academic Provost, but you were
satisfied, more than satisfied as you made clear in your speech accepting
the School of Medicine Dean's Award, saying you were "the luckiest man
in the world," like your hero, Lou Gehrig.*

3/21/08   The vernal equinox. In two days, I will be sixty-seven. When Bob
was diagnosed with stomach cancer on May 5, 2006, he wondered
if he'd ever see another spring. He saw the rest of 2006 and the
spring of 2007. This spring I am alone and today I am angry,
the word "sad" not strong enough, though usually its heavy
monosyllable suffices.

I start to make lunch for myself, the tomato bisque with rice that
Bob liked, but grief rises like bile. I want to fulfill his desires, banal
and profound. I miss being the main source of his delight. Even
taken all together, the people who care about me don't come close
to a thimbleful of his exclusive love.

Driving to visit my cousin Ellen, listening to Bach's *St. Matthew's Passion*, I am swooped up yet again in the details of Bob's final days. This is not a memory of something that happened many months ago. It is happening right now. The blanket around my shoulder. Under Bob's chin. The insistent presence that final absence evokes.

3/22/08 Talking excitedly around Ellen's kitchen table about Barack Obama, about Tom Cruise and Richard Gere, I feel lonesome and uneasy. I'd probably be talking as much if Bob were here, but would he join in? Would he be bored? Would he be looking forward to going home, so we could have the weekend to garden, watch baseball, feed the fish? Was he, as I thought, happy with my volubility and with his own reserve?

3/24/08 I'm enjoying birthday borscht, brisket and bullshit at Sharon and Irv's. I mean bullshit in the best possible sense, the everyday talk about what we like and don't like; do and do not believe; the subject matter serving as an aid to digestion. The gravy, bread, carrot and potatoes are as wonderful as the tender meat. I brought the salad greens. Sharon prepared the toasted almonds, the dressing, and added goat cheese. They sang "Happy Birthday" over a small carrot cake (which we gobbled up, though we knew another friend might be coming over later).

Now it's my responsibility and opportunity to incorporate Bob's strength into myself, including his approbation. He was proud of the time he gave me to write while he read the paper Sunday mornings. Not smug, but proud. We were both aware of that lovely dance of the couple who protects each other's privacy as well as yearning for the company of the other. Some days, even before he got sick, when I worked in my upstairs office, I sensed the emptiness that would follow my not being able to count on his bedrock presence below.

"A joyful mind is very ordinary and relaxed," Pema Chödrön reminds me, and I realize what fun it would have been to share with Bob my sense of him as a Buddhist. He would neither have scorned nor exalted the revelation, though he might have mocked it lightly at a party, and I might have laughed or been uneasy, or both.

3/25/08   I wasn't sure until I was in the car and approaching University Avenue that I would go to the arboretum on such a cold day. The brittle leaves skittered at my feet, rushing past on their own mission. I took the Strasbourg Trail to the Cliff Trail and was rewarded by large rock formations, an explanatory placard about the pawpaw, the shale, the sandstone, the geology of the alluvial plain. On the way around the Guthrie Loop, I noticed several trees dedicated to people's memories.

3/26/08   The rain and chill suit me. I put on a robe rather than turn up the heat. I've taken grapes to bed, delighted as the swiftness of my step causes a breeze to blow away the napkin I've placed on top of them.

I'm reading Daniel Stern's *The Diary of a Baby*, a book I bought for a friend and new mother and kept for myself. How very much like an infant is a person newly alone. No words. No ideas. Feelings are everything, the barrier between inside and outside permeable. "It is not clear [to the baby] how he gets from one moment to the next or what, if anything, happens between them." Grief throws us back to our earliest loneliness, helplessness and deprivation. I read on and make note of the major changes that enter a baby's life with language, about my own reliance on words and my dread of those occasions when they do not suffice.

Agnes is eager to tell me about an encounter she had with Bob's spirit. She flutters her hands to describe how it flew past. She is certain that he was much younger. "That's the way it happens," she assures me. "When they come back, they're younger." And, she adds, my eyes perhaps betraying doubt, "I heard it on TV as well."

3/29/08   I made a good decision: To throw myself out of the house at 4:00 rather than continue the unsatisfying clearing of the cluttered dining room table. I walked the Cliff Trail again, even after yesterday's rain. It was full of just-about-to-open bluebells, the backs of the new leaves already burgundy, the bells tiny and tight, hinting blue.

I'd never been in the arboretum this early in the year. Bob and I often walked toward the middle of April, when the Sheldon Trail was already awash in blue and pink, plants cascading down hillsides. The flowers I saw now were near the road, poking through unpromising layers of soil, fragments of old mining areas. However beautiful, abundance doesn't tell the story of this struggle to begin again, this unlikely persistence and triumph.

April

Fritz Scholder (sp)
    painter of cover of ceremony

She wonders at
the people who help people destroy themselves
including those who sand them—
the Ringing Ghost about Thiure
Kim came & rectuing & the Tamahura   Chihauke (sp?)

        It made her feel happy and free

Collaborative   Chalk pro —— Spanish whore house
work

        When I think about my place on the
        accident in light of what she
        says. I think of the house of care
        Creaking in the back ground and of
        Water Masters starting the fires, warming
        up horned toad god & Toad horns?

    "ways of noticing"
        reverence for the smallest creature
    Something that happened 500 years ago can
    be more important than what happened a
        _ ago.

    ——— seed thought
    A novel could be built   Clerestory
        out of stories.   Story
                                      Stories
    clerestory

Bob
teaching me
how to
[illegible]
the Ghost

4/1/08   April Fool's Day. What a great joke it would be if Bob came back today! I hear something hostile in my thought, not against Bob, but against myself and the whole apparatus of grieving.

4/3/08   I remember the time in my parents' Manhattan apartment when I looked west toward the Hudson River at a sunset that thrilled my heart. I wanted to share it with Bob but was afraid to phone him. We hadn't known each other long and I was afraid to be disappointed by his insufficient response. Or was it by my inability to express what I was feeling? I might have thought—I was young—that I was protecting us both.

I feel I'm waking from the fifty-year dream of my life with Bob, our life together and my life as part of his. The question I ask myself is not who am I without Bob but, more fundamentally, who was I ever?

When, words tumbling, I report to Stephanie all I've been doing, reading, thinking, feeling, she says I am falling in love with myself. I've been insisting, when describing my new energy, that there is no other person involved. But, there is. It's me! I miss Bob and our life together, but I'm discovering things at a speed that would have been impossible were he alive and our life continuing as "normal."

Would you be surprised, Bob, at how "well" I am doing? By the things I can do without you? Or, had you come to see that I would manage?

At least I don't have to tell you about my recent car accident. Not my fault. That woman in the large Cadillac Escalade just kept backing up, claimed she couldn't see me, couldn't hear my horn. It was a bit of a mess for a while. I forgot to call the police. But there was a witness. And I called the insurance company right away. Wouldn't you blame me a little—or is that just me projecting my own insecurity long after you had "upgraded" your estimation of my practical skills?

4/11/08   It's 2:00 a.m. and 62 degrees. Sensing the air with an insect's precision, I do not feel alone. Spring exists without Bob or me, inevitable in its brevity and its recurrence. Not life, not death, but the improbability of one and the inevitability of the other.

I've accepted an invitation to do a workshop for our local lifelong learners' group on comedy and grief. I am not interested in teaching others how to make people laugh, but in helping them to find and cherish their own capacities for incongruity and surprise. I have ample proof that humor is one way of letting go, of not re-creating our old selves.

4/13/08   What will I do in the garden this spring? Will I plant salvia in the containers Bob spray-painted white each year? Will I plant his blood-red cannas, carefully protected over the winter? The elephant ear that delighted us with its improbable size?

Every year, as we sat in the spring garden, Bob said, "This is the best it's ever been." And every year it was true.

When I get my car inspected in May, I will be finished with car obligations for a while. Next year they will be routine; I will have taken over one more of the jobs Bob did for both of us. I consider writing a book for the living, advising them to explore themselves fully and gently for absences and insecurities. I will call it "Advance Directives."

4/17/08   Yesterday I played a tape very loudly in the car and loved the beat going through my body; today when I hear music blasting, as I walk down the street, I feel generous toward the young driver. Then I remember that several years earlier, on a crisp spring day like this, I was accosted by a man's voice, from a music-filled car, screaming, "Die, old woman!"

4/20/08   I've chosen to put a plaque on a dawn redwood, a tree thought to be extinct but, as I read on the arboretum sign, rediscovered in China in the 1940s and related to ancestors of the giant redwoods. It's a deciduous conifer, its feathery needles returning each spring. I want people to remember Bob and what he stood for. He disliked demonstrations and slogans, particularly chanting them. He was wise, gentle, fair and unpretentious. I decided on "In memory of Bob Stitzel, because he cared."

4/26/08   While visiting with David and Laurel in Seattle, I am aware of the stress we all endured during Bob's illness. When David and I take a long walk, I marvel at the size of Northwest flowers, towering tulips and iris, and dandelions almost beautiful, with their toothed leaves tall and upright.

I am renting a car alone for the first time in my life and buying city maps from Elliott Bay Bookstore. Before a new city becomes familiar, it retains an air, simultaneously demure and flirtatious, promising nothing, but suggesting everything.

Wow! I found the downtown Enterprise. Rented a car. Bought insurance. Drove to the Frye Museum. Denny Street to Boren. Missed my turn on James. Found the Frye anyway. Am I for real? I found the button to operate the mirrors. I love my new maps!

I want to live in a house where I can look out on the sea, watch flocks of birds zoom by—an occasional seal or orca. I want the moon, its push and pull, grave and icy white beyond reproach. I want to float in silk robes beyond reach of all but those who know me best. I have a fleeting sense that I am ready to leave this world. Not suicidal. Not in the least. But poised.

May

5/2/08   On a morning after a mostly sleepless night in Seattle, I exhort myself: Remember these things. You felt miserable in the middle of the night. Sad and inadequate, leaning towards anger. You put on the clock radio. You fell asleep again. You felt miserable again when you woke to the radio. Violence in Zimbabwe. Food prices too high. Unemployment. You meditated. You heard Kaya call her dad and heard him respond. You heard Kaya call her mom and heard her answer. Such presence. So much love. It broke your heart wide open.

5/5/08   Laurel showed me how to enter and track items in Quicken. I don't know if I will use it, but it was much less daunting than in November. Could I have learned this from Bob even before he got sick? Could he have offered to explain it to me? Would I have accepted?

At dinner with Laurel's sister Alison and her husband Jamie, I shared my aspirations to write and perform comedy. I also told them what I was learning about living in a couple as I examined my newly single state. Happily, your partner does not have to die for you to realize how little responsibility you took for fulfilling your own desires. In big things and small. For instance, he wasn't the one who always wanted to leave the party early or stay home on a Friday night. She wasn't the one who had doubts about buying that condo, taking that trip. It was you all along, hiding.

On the flight from Seattle to Minneapolis, I felt some chest pain. Something like indigestion, something like muscle strain. I had been writing steadily for several hours, probably with bad posture. Maybe I was hungry, since I felt better after eating. But now, writing in bed, I'm uncomfortable again and remember reading that symptoms of a heart attack are less dramatic for women than for men.

5/8/08   Will I look on this week of homecoming from Seattle as a turning
          point? Another turning point? Every day a turning point? What's
          the origin of that phrase? Ballet? Mountain climbing? Where shall
          I put what feels like new energy? What should I do with these
          hours before seeing Stephanie? What would bring most . . . I stop
          short at the word "comfort." That's not the goal.

          I called my doctor with my symptoms, hoping he'd tell me not to
          worry, that it was nothing, but he says he'll have his assistant set up
          an appointment for an EKG.

          I've definitely scheduled too many trips over the next two months.
          I am worried more than I need be over a scandal at the university.
          Should I write a letter to the editor? I'm good at that. I'm afraid
          I may be using my trips to run away from writing and grieving.
          Stephanie doesn't disagree, though she's kinder to me than I am.

5/11/08   I called Elke about my trip to Sweden this summer. I also called
          Pelle and was moved by how easily he understood my need to have
          him and Anna-Karin as backup if Elke's health deteriorated while I
          was staying with her.

          Bob and Mary appeared with a gorgeous Boston fern for Mother's
          Day, which cheered me enormously.

5/13/08   The afternoon was difficult. I exercised at 4:00. But before that, I
          floundered. That word seems perfect for my inability to get a purchase
          on any idea, or action, or feeling; going from room to room, getting
          in and out of bed, avoiding work on an essay I'm writing about that
          car accident Bob never knew about.

This is the spring Bob did not live to see, though he saw two more than we at first thought possible. Across from me, the poppies he'd been waiting for have finally bloomed. In the late afternoon, lady's mantle, sedum, lily fronds, iris blades all yearn toward chartreuse, and the brown tips of spent daffodils glow. When the sun is almost gone and colors can flatten like a face behind splayed fingers, at just the right angle, the white stripes of a hosta dazzle.

5/18/08

Driving to Ohio to spend time with Maggie and Anna, I listen to some of Bob's favorite tapes—Dylan Thomas, Winston Churchill, Monty Python—and feel him with me, admiring "A Child's Christmas in Wales," moved by Churchill's courage, laughing at Python's best sketches: the gumbies, the Spanish Inquisition, exploding penguins.

At Maggie and Anna's, I realize I still want to be taken care of, cooked for, comforted, assured I can write the book I want to, or the essay, or the stand-up schtick. These friends would be fully available to me as they were for weeks, even months, after Bob died, but now that I am ostensibly better and they face the necessities of their own lives, I want more and am ashamed of my greed. After all, even I leave my mourning self behind for hours at a time.

Yet, I also miss the easy comforts and discomforts of long and loving coupledom. "Have you seen my …?" "Where did you put my …?" "Can I help with that?" I miss the series of stepping-stones between past and future, that often unappreciated waystation between now and never again. A life together.

5/20/08   I have a heart scan and a stress test. I'm more tired at the end of the treadmill session than I expected, even a little faint. But I recover quickly and the technician says I've done well. I remember how proud Bob was of his "good numbers," his heart scan, his blood pressure, his hemoglobin. My poor, sweet husband, working so hard to be well and dying anyway.

My friend Ami said that some time after her husband died—she's not sure exactly how long it took—she stopped saying hello to him when she came home. After that she didn't feel so sad. I don't want to stop yet. I don't want it to stop being sad yet.

Ami remembered how well Bob looked in his silk shirt when we had dinner at her home. He said he knew how he wanted to die— a bullet from a jealous husband. At first I'd been surprised that someone of her sensibility would find such a lame joke funny. But she may have thought he was laughing at himself, his macho remarks coming, as they did, from a 70-year-old man who knew he was dying, sooner rather than later.

I think about Bob's mild flirtations with the many women who enjoyed his company and whom he enjoyed. Were those flirtations comfortable only when contained within the circle of our marriage? Would he have been surprised by his own popularity and enjoyed it were I the one to die first?

5/23/08   Change is taking place all around me. My favorite service station may close. The man who cleans my house has had a heart attack. I still don't have the results of my heart test. Who would take me to the hospital if I needed to go? Should I move to Seattle? How long will my children be saddled with an aging, aching mom? It could be twenty-three years if I live as long as my mother and father did.

Preparing to throw away old issues of *The Chronicle of Higher Education*, I see Bob's red checkmarks in the new book section and I can't continue. I'd forgotten how over the years he checked books he thought I'd be interested in—first, women's studies, then lesbian studies, cultural studies, Jewish studies—changing as I changed and respecting what I cared about. He always had me in mind.

Yesterday I denied myself my morning coffee to see if that omission would quiet the intermittent pains in my chest, but the pain came anyway and scared the hell out of me. This morning, I decided I didn't like the sick person I was becoming, so I chose coffee and meditation as my medicine. Like Yogi Berra, I came to a fork in the road and I took it. I went to Lowe's. I bought caladium plants and nasturtium seeds, but I didn't like any of their flabby impatiens. Today I plan to look farther afield at Hillside Gardens and Southern States.

5/24/08   The young man duplicating a house key at the hardware store looked exhausted. I asked him if he'd been partying. But it was his cats, scared by the impending storm and using his body as a raceway. It cheered us both to talk about what cats know that we don't.

After a Saturday of errands, such as one I might have spent with Bob, I realize that I am not afraid of going home without a plan. Maybe for the first time since he died, I feel I can risk leisure and face an open expanse of time.

The medical tests came back negative.

June

6/2/08   I'm very glad I decided to attend Marianne and Andreas's wedding. The black, red and yellow German flag flies benignly in the yard next to their house. The orange poppies, brash and nonchalant, grow from the compost. My journal pages flip in the breeze as if they were trying out for a "B" movie. Marianne and Andreas care for me as they would a valued elder or honored guest. The say again and again how glad they are I've made the long trip.

Nowhere do I feel more Jewish than in Germany. It's not about being a victim. I am not afraid. In fact, I feel braver than usual, like an escaped convict unwilling to give up a life of crime regardless of the consequences.

I've returned from a walk through history and identity, towards the cathedral, past wineries, roses and doves. Did the Jews smell roses on the way to their extinction? Or, did they remember the smell only later, unable to identify its source—confused, as we sometimes are when we greet someone warmly whom we'd forgotten for a moment that we hated?

I imagine myself with a gold star on my arm walking down a modern street in Oppenheim. What would such behavior evoke in these good people? Who would be my friends and who my enemies? When I look at the reliefs in the cathedral, at the gentlemen and their honored wives, with their hands folded neatly in front of them, I imagine them bowing and saying, "*Namaste.*"

While sitting in the church garden, it occurs to me that Bob would have enjoyed the walk, but would not have enjoyed sitting for as long as I did, nor would I have enjoyed my walking meditation if he sat and watched me, however sympathetically.

Had we been in the German garden together we would have congratulated ourselves on the garden to which we would return. Being here with Bob would not have been better, nor worse, but different. "*Nicht rechts, nicht links, aber geradeaus*"—not right, not left, but straight ahead—as the crossing guard said when I asked for directions earlier in the day.

I don't call myself the mother of the bride, but Marianne and I are both aware that in some ways I play that role, since her mother does not approve of her secular wedding. At least I'm here for the important last-minute details, such as what earrings to wear.

6/3/08   When I awake tomorrow morning, it will be my wedding anniversary. Forty-seven years. And we knew each other for four years before that. I assure Marianne and Andreas that despite my sorrow I am happy to be with them, comfortable in their living room where I feel I could stay forever, or at least in the deep cocoon of now.

Bob died at 70 and a half. Yves St. Laurent died today at 71. Trudy in Ursula Hegi's *Stones From the River* is aware that the date of her death is already somewhere in her future. As is mine. And until then? After heavy rain and thunder last night, the sun shines intermittently. I'm enjoying a second piece of dark bread with cottage cheese and cold coffee.

Being with Marianne as she prepares for her wedding allows me to remember the way my mother participated only grudgingly in mine; she came to love Bob in later years and Bob, bless his heart, never held her doubts against her.

When I think of Marianne and Andreas walking home together after the wedding dinner, I envy them the fact of their future, even more than their happiness.

I like all the extravagant promises people make at the end of visits, still aglow in the adventures they've just had. It doesn't matter how many come to fruition. Possibility is what matters.

6/9/08   Back home again, and all is well. The intermingled white and purple clematis are blooming. The bullfrogs are loud. Yes, the dehumidifier isn't working and the basement smells musty. But I'm calm and gentle with myself. Will I unpack before listening to phone messages? Open the mail? Do the laundry? Replacing "I should do this or that" with "Will I?" creates a space in which I hear myself.

6/16/08   We're not going to be able to replace the ceiling windows in the sunroom after all. But Mark has a solution. He can replace the glass with wood, add more interesting lighting. We can start fresh.

I couldn't get the car out of gear this morning. I tried again, which sometimes did the trick when Bob did it. Not this time. Then, much to my surprise, I read the manual and didn't give up when I couldn't immediately find something describing my problem. When I found the instructions and followed them—bless my soul—the damn thing turned over. I begin to understand how terrific Bob felt when he got things to work!

At a retirement party for one of his colleagues, Bob is praised often and warmly. Someone mentioned how well he had looked when last they saw him. I'm stopped short. Will I die? Even when I looked so well the previous March? She died? No way! Get out of here! She looked so good.

6/18/08   I visit Ted and Rosie in Minneapolis where Bob and I got our Ph.Ds and where David was born. Bob and Ted were in the same graduate program almost forty years ago and the four of us traveled together, to France, Ireland, Italy—and Greece. I'm thrown back to Bob's tripping on the rug we bought in Mykonos. I remember how pleased he was he hadn't hurt himself badly, for my sake more than for his own.

Rosie and I drove around the university campus. I wanted to see Nicholson Hall where Bob had dropped me off to meet my freshman English class when I overslept one day and it was too late for me to walk. Students were already pouring out of the building, since according to rule, or legend, they had to wait only five minutes, unless it was for a professor. I was a graduate assistant. "Wait, wait for me," I shouted as I ran toward them—and they did. Bob and I were both astounded.

We looked at photo albums from our trips, memories bubbling up from the images: the time Ted and I crashed a concert during intermission in Wales, Bob's hair longer than mine in an early photo, playbills reminding me how much Bob loved the National Theatre in London. We flipped through pages, stopping every once in a while to reach out for the reassurance of a smile or a touch.

6/21/08   Speaking as a nurse and mother, Rosie's daughter Rosalinda tells me how much worse it is to lose a child at birth than after struggling as she and Eric did throughout the years before he died. "You lose your dreams when you lose a child," she says, "and when the child dies even before you can say hello and goodbye, before you can see him become a self, at least a little, you are trapped in a permanent longing, an impossible hope."

6/23/08   Rosie, Ted and I went to see *A Midsummer Night's Dream* at the Tyrone Guthrie Theater, which opened in 1963, the year Bob and I moved to Minneapolis. It was fantastic, literally and metaphorically. The timing, the self-parody, the willingness to dare and play and risk, all made me want to whoop and yell in gratitude. It was a song of imagination drunk on its own grave purpose, a purpose meant to cheat the grave, at least for a while.

On the plane home, I long for Bob. Enough already, I hear myself say out loud. You've been dead long enough. Come home!

6/24/08   I will bring Bob's ashes to Marstrand, Sweden, to have a ceremony there with David, Laurel and Kaya. We will return to his favorite view from the rocky terrain where he quipped he wanted us to roll him if he was ever in a wheelchair. Based on her own experience with her sister's ashes, my therapist gave me some tips. They're heavier than you might imagine. They're not like dust and won't blow away. There may be pieces of bone.

As I turned a corner on a walk to think about preparing the ashes for travel, a young deer leapt out of the woods and across my path onto a large, open expanse where it stopped abruptly. A woman drove by slowly, saw me, saw the deer, and waved. A man drove towards us from a side road, looked out his truck window and said, with what sounded like wonder, "He's not afraid of you." Then he took a picture with his cell phone. As he drove away, I said, "Good evening," as if the confluence of woman, deer and man deserved some benediction. The deer remained still for a while after the man drove away, as if unable to make up its mind where to go next. Then it disappeared into the small woodland where it had come from. When I told Loana about the deer, she said, "Grief makes our boundaries porous and animals feel safe when our benign energy invites them in."

Bob and I never anticipated a time when I would be handling his ashes. Even writing that sentence feels bizarre. But I needed a ritual and made one in our garden's gazebo. Upon opening the unassuming plastic box, I saw a mesa, gray hills sloping to a wide expanse. Some crevices were deeper than others, but none were forbidding. Picking the larger pieces from the small, I felt like I did as a child, playing with my mother's hair, amazed that I was allowed this intimacy. I washed my face with the dust, and the scent—clean, fresh and ancient—comforted me. It smelled like eternity. I could imagine making something lovely from these remnants.

I separated the ashes into baggies, each with a hollyhock, Bob's favorite flower; one each for Kaya, David, Laurel and me; two more for Pelle and Anna-Karin. Then I spread some ashes near Bob's poppies and saved the rest to be mixed with mine.

6/25/08   I'm as flustered and unsettled today as I was at peace yesterday. Too many things to accomplish before I leave—buying a new camera, seeing the dentist, meeting with a financial advisor. Where are all the papers I need for that meeting? I'm tired of all this independence.

6/30/08   I'm in Bob's study to spend time with him before I leave
            for Sweden.

            I can't throw out the reprints of his scientific papers. I tried, then
            took them out of the wastepaper basket. I remember the trouble
            I had convincing him to bring them home from his office, and I
            feel tears when I see the three-ring binders and colored paper we
            bought to allow him to preserve them. He had little enthusiasm for
            the task, but he humored me on the trip to the craft store. After all,
            wasn't this the kind of thing one was supposed to do in retirement?
            Was it for my sake that he endured this ridiculous stay of execution?

            The reprints move me in their own right. All those combinations
            of names, those cooperative ventures, going back to Augusto Campos,
            his graduate school advisor; Fred Shideman, his straitlaced chairman
            in Minnesota, and Pelle Lundborg, the Swedish colleague I'll be
            visiting. I feel terrific when it occurs to me I can frame a reprint for
            Pelle as a gift. More than ever, I admire the delight Bob took in
            his research, the careful calibrations, the necessary repetitions, the
            satisfying results.

            I remember helping Bob revise a manuscript. We're in the kitchen,
            in our house, in Minneapolis. I think David was already born—
            though this is exactly the kind of detail I cannot easily corroborate
            without Bob. We may have been working on a draft of his dissertation
            and Bob was reading something out loud. Perhaps about dopamine.
            I didn't understand the science, but I could tell that some transition
            was missing whose inclusion would make his case stronger. I
            remember that Bob agreed and that I felt smart, proud and useful.

Coming upon the charts we kept to record fluctuations in Bob's medications and weight, I remember how proud we were when the cancer center nutritionist complimented us and praised his balanced diet. Greens. Proteins. Ensure. Potassium. Gleefully I noted every 1/2 lb. gained, worried over every 1/2 lb. lost. Will I throw them out before I die? I want David, who designed them, to find them and to remember the excellent care I gave his father.

My mood is changing, now, as if coming out of the trance-like state that working in Bob's study enabled. I saved everything that will enable me to enter that state whenever I want to.

July

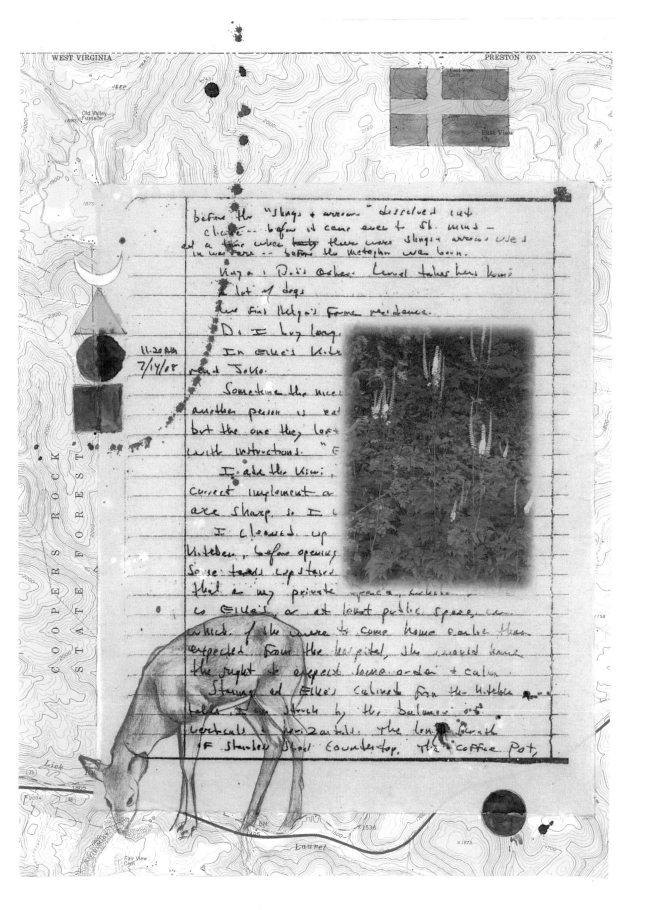

before the "slings + arrows" dissolved into
cliché -- before it came even to Sh. mins --
at a time when there were slings+ arrows used
in warfare -- before the metaphor was born.

Kaya + D.'s Oshas. Laurel takes here home
a lot of dogs
her first Helga's former residence.

D. I buy long.

11:20 AM   In Elke's Kitchen
7/14/08 read JoKo.

Sometimes the nicest
another person is eat
but the one they loof
with instructions. "E

I ate the kiwi,
correct implement or
are sharp, so I u

I cleaned up
Kitchen, before opening
Some tools upstairs
that in my private space, whereas
is Elke's, or at least public space, in
which if she were to come home earlier than
expected from the hospital, she would have
the right to expect home-order + calm.

Staring at Elke's cabinet from the kitchen
table, I am struck by the balance of
verticals + horizontals. The long beneath
of Stainless Steel Countertop, the coffee pot,

7/1/08   Last night working at the kitchen table on finances, I imagined
          the face of an intruder behind the sliding-glass patio doors. What
          would I do? Run out the front door, even without my shoes? And
          if there were assassins outside the front door as well, what then? I'd
          be killed. Terrified and then dead.

          My appointment with Joseph for a pre-trip pedicure was disappointing.
          He was tired and inattentive. I know he works seven days a week,
          trying to make it in the U. S., having come here from Vietnam. But
          I needed more from him. The pizza at the mall's Sbarro's was cold
          and the cheese congealed, but not until now did I remember that
          my first Sbarro meal was at the Newark airport. I still didn't know
          that soon I'd be on a bus to the SAS plane and the beginning of the
          birthday extravaganza in Sweden that Bob and Elke had planned
          over the past year. How ever did they keep it a surprise for so long?

7/2/08   Oh no! I need a root canal before I leave for Sweden. At the
          endodontist, I swing between distrust ($1,000, he's got to be
          kidding) and sycophancy ("Oh, thank you, thank you so much,
          for fitting me in before I leave").

          Chilling out at Starbucks. I'm still not completely packed but feel
          as if my vacation has begun. I have made the necessary phone calls,
          prepared all the computer backups, double-checked that my
          passport is up-to-date. Something has let go.

7/4/08   If I had thrown out the broken videotape of *Big Night*, one of Bob's favorite films, I would not have remembered how happy he was to have found a used copy for $6.50 so he could share it with me. Or how much pleasure he took when I found something funny even when he didn't. He loved my unexpected laughter, as I was moved by his delight in *Out of Africa*; how he would say, in concert with Meryl Streep, "I had a farm in Africa, at the foot of the Ngong Hills." What exactly was he feeling that came out in that husky, tear-washed voice?

I also remember how angry he was when the VCR player ate *Big Night* and one other tape. What were we arguing about? That we shouldn't have bought that particular VCR to begin with? That I was going to return it to Best Buy and insist we get our warranty honored, even though it was out-of-date? I haven't a clue anymore.

7/5/08   There are delays at the airport. Finally, a flight attendant's voice: "Let me welcome our first-class passengers onto the plane." When she comes back for the rest of us, she offers no welcome but announces that seating area B is now available for boarding. She has released the rabble from her proprietary embrace.

7/8/08   I started to cry as soon as I saw the edge of the Swedish archipelago, the sea, the rocks, the red-roofed yellow houses. When the wheels touched down at Landvetter Airport in Gothenburg, I pronounced Bob officially dead.

Thank goodness David, Laurel and Kaya have joined me here. We had a delicious day together, including getting lost on our walk around the city. A lovely couple stopped as we fiddled with the map on the way back to Pelle's apartment where they were staying. "You look like you know where you're going," the man said encouragingly. "Just not the best way to get there."

Elke is the "benevolent hurricane" Bob lovingly dubbed her, and, even with Göte's death four years earlier and her own recent diagnosis of chronic leukemia, she has lost little of her vibrancy. But the second night I was with her, she woke unable to breathe. I'm not sure how, but I stayed calm enough to follow instructions to get an ambulance to take her to a hospital. It was pneumonia.

At her home without her the next day, I walked slowly through the stately, inviting spaces, letting the memories of over thirty years wash over me. I ended in the parlor where, on the eve of my fiftieth birthday, I sat on the elegant settee with Elke's mother, Helga, as David and Laurel and our Swedish friends entered from the floor below, smiling mischievously as their presence revealed the surprise Bob and Elke had been plotting for months.

7/15/08   Weeks before we came, Elke had reserved rooms for us at Carlsten Castle. This seventeenth-century fortress was now a guesthouse, and we had come to scatter Bob's ashes on our beloved Marstrand Island. Together, David, Laurel, Kaya and I walked along the stony path to find a view we agreed was most likely the one Bob had pointed out years before, not far from where bay became sea, but where it was still calm enough for people and red-roofed cottages as well as screaming gulls. It was drizzling, and we missed the crisp blue sky we loved, but we agreed the soft grey was better for our ceremony.

"You can't do it wrong," I said, and Laurel told me later that my assurances had been welcome. I scattered my bag of ashes among the pebbles at my feet. David walked far enough away to be invisible to me, perhaps to the water's edge; perhaps remembering how, as a child, he ran among these rocks under his father's eye. Laurel, like me, stood where she was and said she'd like to take the ashes home with her, if that was all right. Kaya, who had never been to Marstrand, was the most adventurous, scampering away with her plastic bag in hand, frightening us all with her speed, but coming back safely and whole. Later Laurel remarked that, of course, Kaya would want to be alone with Bob, as she had been during their last time together at our pond.

7/20/08   What's going on? Today I am anxious to go home without seeing the rest of my friends. I'd be on a plane to Pittsburgh in a minute if Bob would come with me. I'd let him choose whether to forget the whole dead business and start from where we were or whether he'd want me to fill him in on what he'd missed. What would he want to know? Would he be as tickled as I am by how much Anna-Karin and Pelle's relationship mirrors ours in big ways and small? The way Pelle skillfully fixes perennially loose screws in her glasses? The way Anna-Karin drives from the backseat?

Pelle, Anna-Karin and I had dinner in an inn both rustic and refined, where I felt privileged to pay. To cap off our meal, we ordered dessert tapas, a magnificent sextet of delicious concoctions: A crème brûlée with herbs; *kalvdans* (dancing calf), the first milk of a recently-delivered cow; cloudberries and ice cream; nuts and honey; chocolate mousse and strawberries. I remember the beauty and playfulness of the six glasses set in front of us. Driving home, each of us told the others, as if it were our own secret, that we had felt Bob with us throughout the meal.

7/23/08   Yesterday we buried some of Bob's ashes near the lake down the hill from Pelle and Anna-Karin's cottage. We were at the spot we'd scouted out the previous night, a scrubby hillock, surrounded by oak seedlings and bluebells; by pebbles and sand left behind by the last Ice Age. When I told them about washing my face with the ashes, Pelle bent close and agreed that they smelled of eternity. They dug two holes, but the earth Anna-Karin had chosen seemed more friable; so they mixed their ashes together to make it more likely the hollyhock would bloom.

Pelle told me that he would never forget that Bob "provided the platform" for his own scientific career, and Anna-Karin said how sorry she was we never made that trip to Spain we often talked about.

I imagine traveling the world with Bob's ashes in my arms.

7/31/08   Home again! Home again! Several times while I was away I had the thought I'd like to refresh the house when I returned. I've begun to accumulate rather than cherish. I'd like to see cleaner lines, own fewer objects that I no longer use.

August

8/1/08   At first I thought I hadn't shaken some sand out of my shoes, but,
            no, the remaining ashes I carried home had sifted through their
            cardboard container and into the crevices of my suitcase.

            Guess it's out of the bag! Though I love these ashes, I do not
            revere them. When I told Stephanie that I found them beautiful
            and thought of putting them in a bowl, she suggested a container
            with a lid would be safer.

8/3/08   I was uneasy during Micki's visit. Last year when she was here, she
            had been planning to stay at our house while we were at a reunion
            of Bob's college classmates. But then he developed a blood clot
            and couldn't travel. I told her to come anyway, with her sweet pug,
            whose company Bob usually enjoyed. But he was too tired for the
            dog's affectionate antics.

8/4/08   Maybe next year, I won't be so disorganized. I'll be in Bob's study,
            rearranged as my financial office, but now I've spread papers out
            on the kitchen table with the chairs surrounding me and the floor
            serving as an ancillary desk. Have I made out the estate tax checks
            correctly? For state and federal taxes? I mustn't forget stamps and
            return addresses and forms for certified mail receipts.

8/6/08   Dream: I'm at the graduation ceremony for my MFA degree. We're
            picking up documents that contain comments and photos taken
            by our fellow students. I'm disappointed with the generic remarks.

They're like those you might find in a high school yearbook—
"Love you forever," "You're the best." I'm sure the farewell messages
others received were more detailed and complimentary.

My God, I feel alone!

In another dream, I must jump over an empty space from one flat
rock to another. The space isn't very large, the leap manageable, but
I'm afraid of what I may be leaving behind.

8/7/08   I make plans to visit Sylvia Washton and her children on Whidbey
Island and then David and his family to exchange tales of our
summer travels. The Washtons knew my mother and father before
I was born, through my childhood and beyond. I want to wrap
myself in the intimacy of early memories as I get close to the
anniversary of Bob's death.

An actor friend has offered to do a reading at a local theater based
on selections from my master's thesis, *The Junk Dealer's Daughter*.
How much do I want to be involved in the actual production?
What will best serve my art? I feel pretentious asking myself that
question. Yet proud as well; I'm becoming my own best friend.

I had an elegant lunch at Ami's house, where I was treated as an
honored guest by her and Tachen. We ate imported mackerel, five
slim fish, looking like large sardines, with their eyes wide open.
Tachen stood each mackerel on its side, tapped it firmly along its
back and filleted it in a flash. We had a salad of light mayonnaise
and cucumbers fresh from the garden. I almost ate some cat food,
thinking it was an unusual Japanese snack.

Bob and Tachen always greeted each other by bowing. "I'm ready for dessert now," Bob would say in Japanese, whatever the occasion. It was a phrase from the tea ceremony Tachen had taught us many years before, and which he never forgot.

8/8/08

What if I had only one day to live? Would I garden or organize things for my children? Nothing wrong with the second impulse. But if it was truly 24 (or even 48 or 96) hours? I'd stay in the Now, with the pond, the fish, the screeching crow; with the young black koi turning orange, its pursed lips white, like paint on a clown's face. These late summer days I've been taking away dead branches and yellowing seed pods, from yarrow, iris, betony and spiderwort. Deadheading, I'm making room for beauty.

Reading *The New Yorker* at the pond, I find Thomas Wentworth Higginson writing about Emily Dickinson: "There may be years of crowded passion in a word, and half a life in a sentence." I read the first poem she sent him with its verb/noun mysteries—*row, drop, surrender*—and think that verbs must occasionally yearn for the stasis of nouns.

I check Amazon for a book about Buddhism to bring for Kaya. It's never too early to become familiar with a tradition that allows us to observe our emotions and thoughts rather than be in thrall to them. I think Bob had a meditation practice, though he wouldn't have called it that. Watching the Yankees on TV, he'd carefully spread newspapers across the carpet and polish his ancient and comfortable shoes.

Going through the day's mail, I enjoy sorting things to recycle, to throw away, and to put aside to deal with later, like the Lands' End catalogue which included that model Bob particularly admired. Sometimes he bought entire outfits the guy wore—down to his shoes and ties.

Bob's clothes, his favorite shirt and ties, tug at me. It's silly to ask what good do your clothes do you now? But that question comes, sheathing one more unsettling? What does any of it—not just our possessions—avail any of us? I feel his vulnerability, not only during those last days, but his vulnerability as a man, my husband, a mortal. His sweetness. His kindness. An ache he had I might never have known about. An ache he had I may have caused.
I want him back. I want his humor, his support and affirmation, his wit and his balance. I want to watch the Yankees with my head on his lap, his hand in my hair, the two of us.

8/13/08   I've had a thrilling Japanese lesson to prepare me for a visit to Suzanne in November. Not only a new language, but a new set of shapes to embody it. And within those shapes a new way of being and seeing. Yaeko, my teacher, said I was very good, which I didn't believe for a minute, some of the sounds eluding me entirely. But I was taking delight not only in being a good student, but in recognizing the differences in the ways in which Japanese and Americans negotiate the appropriate ways in which to enter another's life. *Excuse me. Just a moment. Sorry. Forgive me for being rude. May I be of service?*

Some acquaintances I haven't seen for a while are very happy to greet me. I could see that plainly in their bright smiles. They had a category to put me in—recovering nicely. When I talk soon after with Sherry, she agrees that we will not be ready for the world of normal expectations after the one-year anniversary of our husbands' deaths. We wonder about expiration dates and renewals for grieving. "Like a license plate," she suggests.

I got an answer to a letter I wrote to Pema Chödrön. It wasn't from Pema herself, but from Louise St. Marie, the Gambo Abbey correspondent who writes that Ani Pema is in silent retreat, but "she would want me to send you her love and appreciation for taking her teachings to heart and for taking the time to let her know."

8/14/08   A surprising new sadness has pooled into an ink stain on my table cloth. An oil stain appears on my driveway. I could have cried in my tiny manicurist's arms. I left a more than usually needy message on my niece Maria's answering machine.

It's a year since the last two weeks of August—Bob on the downslide, fluid pooling in his intestines. *Can we go to bed now?*

Is there something I'm not doing in preparation for this anniversary? I told David that I thought I was doing okay, that there were some financial things I thought it would be good to have taken care of, such as finally putting accounts in my name, but that I was not going to make myself crazy over artificial deadlines. That feels right, but I still may be missing something. I return to unfinished business in my beloved's study. Not the language I usually use—beloved. But there it is.

I throw away and then retrieve the yellow page covered with plant names, some in my handwriting, some in Bob's, some—the ones he had already made labels for—crossed out in red pen. There's a note about caring for the ajuga: any kind of well-drained soil, full shade to full sun. Neither one of us had reckoned on its being destroyed by the creatively-invasive chameleon plant.

Once again, I encounter the inadequacies of his things. None of them kept him alive. Not the poster of Alice Springs sent by a colleague, not the oversized cardboard check to commemorate a large donation he arranged for the medical center, not the photo of me at sixteen when we met.

8/15/08   Agnes and Paul brought me a beautiful bouquet. They remembered how pained they were to see Bob lying on the chaise a year ago, too tired to greet them. "You're family," Agnes says. "Don't forget that. Call us if you need us." The whole time we talked, Micki's pug Chaska, usually unable to resist a lap, sat quietly next to us. She seemed to recognize our solemn mood.

"He left me," I say to Micki, as we look at photos together. "He didn't want to," she says. I love her for it.

When my therapist first talked about "goneness," I recoiled at the word, but recently when Loana said, "It's hard to believe that someone can be that gone," I wrote it down. "When someone dies," she continued, "abstract mortality is backlit by their concrete goneness." Apparently, grief requires its own syntax and vocabulary.

8/17/08   Maggie suggests kindly that I may only now be feeling what I couldn't feel a year before, so focused was I on *doing*. That sounds right to me. I tell her how aware David and I are of Bob's presence, as if these weeks before September are our last chance for us to turn back time, to make real our strong sensation that what happened didn't happen, that he didn't die. Maggie says she's heard that after a year something changes. It's not that we miss the person less, but that they let go. The deer returns into the bushes, beyond which there may be a clearing, and leaves us behind, but whole.

8/18/08   My old, old friend Harriet is dying. A mutual friend called to prepare me. Micki and I agree that at our age we must get used to our friends dying. But before 70! Please!!!!

Today's session with Stephanie was startling in its intensity. As I sobbed, huddled in my chair across from her, she said that I had not been in this place before. Except for moments with Maggie and Anna and with David and Laurel, I had, in some sense, put my mourning for Bob on hold. Here it was in full force.

Stephanie cautions me to be careful. She tells me that within the first 18 months of a major loss, 85% of people get sick or have an accident. I'm skeptical. I wonder whether within *any* 18-month period, 85% of all people get sick or have an accident.

8/19/08   I found the text for Bob's speech ending "I'm the luckiest man in the world" and the dinner speech he gave for a colleague's graduate students. The former moved me to tears. The latter, which I didn't attend—well, in the latter, he talked about remaining in New York for his MA so I could finish my BA. He attributed his delay to "raging hormones." At first, I was uneasy with his "exposing" me as a sexual object and himself as an old man talking about sex. Then I was ashamed of my prudishness.

I call Harriet's sister Renée to tell her how sad I am; we comfort each other even though we haven't seen each other or talked for years. Renée imagines Bob and Harriet meeting in heaven and their likely conversation: "We didn't believe and they let us in anyway. What a hoot!" It was good to laugh with her. Recently I spoke with Stephanie about missing Bob's irreverence. How at the end of one of the email messages I sent friends about his illness, he had insisted I add, on his behalf, "I approve this message."

8/22/08   Buddhists tell the story of a person—sometimes a woman, sometimes a man—who is caught on a precipice, tigers above, tigers below, with a mouse gnawing on the rope between. The person notices a beautiful strawberry in a crevice, removes it and savors it. Moments before Bob died, I became aware that dopamine was being used to raise his plummeting blood pressure. Amazed, I told the nurses that dopamine was the first drug he had used in his experiments as a graduate student. "What did you do?" a nurse asked him. "I'm a pharmacologist," he answered, fully present, embracing the work he loved. When I told Stephanie this story, she gave me a gift. "How remarkably in tune you were," she said. "You allowed him to taste that strawberry."

8/25/08   How can I possibly feel unloved with so many caring friends? I don't. But I feel unknown in the profound way Bob knew me. I was the only person, except David, whom he dreaded leaving, without whom he might not want to live. Of course, he, too, would have continued. Might he have fallen in love again? Would he remember our song "When I fall in love, it will be forever…"?

I had already inserted Ramsey Lewis into the car's tapedeck, increased the volume and started to "dance" in my seat, when I remembered the advice our landscaper gave when we had our yard torn up following a destructive leak: "Don't put things back the way they were. There's no dishonor to what you had before, or to how much you loved it, to try something new. You have a clean slate."

Maybe not so clean. For, when I accomplish something as routine as printing out a boarding pass, I recall the way Bob would have done it—for us—and my heart empties.

Acknowledgments

Many people have sustained me. Some of them you have already met, such as Maggie Anderson, always my best teacher; Anna French, whose wisdom matched her nurturing; Sharon and Irv Goodman and Stephanie Savitch, who were with me in my hardest hours. There were some, like Natasha Sajé, Susan Sailer, Than Saffel, Susan Shumaker and Rae Jean Sielen, who read my pages at critical junctures. Dee Quaranto kept me steady and smiling, Micki Ginsberg and Marianne Ebend traveled miles to be with me, and old friends of Bob called often and never got off the phone without saying, "Remember that we love you." There are cherished others who I trust know my deep gratitude though I have not named them here.

I am grateful to my teachers and colleagues at Vermont College and to the staff and fellows at the Virginia Center for the Creative Arts. Because of them I could stretch far and feel joy, even as I learned to say goodbye.

Artist's Note

About five years ago, Judith approached me about collaborating on a journal project focusing on her garden. I didn't reject the idea, but I wasn't quite sure about it either. I was always a little leery of collaborations—not quite sure that I wanted to subsume my artistic voice in another's vision.

A couple of years later, her husband Bob was very sick, and although I felt terrible for what he was going through, it was Judith's experience as his caregiver that touched me deeply. She told me she was keeping a journal of these feelings and experiences, and after Bob died, we brought up the idea of collaboration again.

I felt that something very positive and healing might come out of this project, so I began to experiment with formats and to think about what approach the images might take. Early on, I was intrigued by the idea that a journal is a "book of days." Creating an image for each calendar month seemed like a workable structure in which to present my responses to Judith's words.

Judith and I were both clear that I wasn't going to "illustrate" her journal. I did read it and sometimes took images from her writing. I printed actual pages from her journal as part of each month's imagery. Judith is *in* each picture, but they are not *about* her and Bob.

Combining different media in the images—printmaking, photography, drawing and collage—is typical of my work. I used geological survey maps to create a sense of place and grounding. Transfer prints of Judith's journal pages on Japanese paper were glued on top of the maps. Digital photographs were taken during each month and printed on Japanese paper. Plants, animals, words in different alphabets and shapes relate to the time of year or Judith's writing in a kind of free association.

As friends, Judith and I share a great deal: a love of art and writing, and an interest in Buddhism, nature and gardening. The process of creating this book with her has blurred the line for me between receiving and giving. My hope is that you the reader/viewer will be touched by this gift as well.

I would like to thank Shannon Knepper for her wonderful design that makes both Judith's and my work shine; and Nan Newell for proofreading the text. For assistance with creating the images, many thanks to the staff at Artists Image Resource; and for their spiritual and artistic support I am most grateful to my fellow artists at Saranam art retreats, where I made many of these works.

Claudia Giannini

Judith Gold Stitzel is a retired professor of English and Women's Studies at West Virginia University where she and her husband Bob started their teaching careers in 1965 and where she was the founding director of the WVU Center for Women's Studies. She has published fiction, non-fiction and literary criticism in *Colorado Quarterly*, *Frontiers, a Journal of Women Studies*; *College English*; *Green Mountain Review;* and other journals and anthologies. She has an MFA in creative writing from Vermont College and has twice been a fellow at the Virginia Center for the Creative Arts. She lives in Morgantown, West Virginia.

Claudia Giannini holds an M. Ed. in museum education and has worked in the museum field since 1981. She received her MFA degree from West Virginia University in 1999, with specialization in printmaking and photography. She has held residencies at the Vermont Studio Center and Virginia Center for Creative Arts and participated in a residency at Artists Image Resource in Pittsburgh sponsored by the Mid-Atlantic Arts Foundation. Claudia has exhibited her work widely in galleries throughout the country, and her work is included in public and private collections.